My God and I

A True Story of Love, Music, Death, and Faith

 Bobby Denton

Cover design and interior format
Clayton Mitchell

Printed in the United States of America
by **Lambert Book House**
Florence, Alabama

ISBN 978-1-68489-607-3

FALLEN STAR
PUBLISHING

Dedication

I dedicate this book to "Sweetie" my dear friend
and long-time companion.

Chapter One

"Love is patient and kind; love is not jealous or boastful; it is not arrogant or rude; love does not insist on its own way; it is not enviable or resentful; it does not rejoice at wrong, but rejoices in the right; love bears all things; believes all things; hopes all things; and endures all things" (1 Corinthians 13:4–8). The scriptures say that God knew us while we were still in our mothers' wombs. It is hard to comprehend the power of God and His love for us. He can see the future and even knows the intentions of our hearts. Being human, it is impossible for us to know the mind of God. We cannot comprehend the term omnipotent. All knowing can only be comprehended through our faith in God. God knows everything that is occurring everywhere at all times and even knows the number of hairs on our heads.

Saturday, August 13, 1938, was a hot and steamy summer day. In the late afternoon, the pains of childbirth could be heard all around the little house on a rocky hillside seven miles south of Cherokee, Alabama, on White Pike Road near the Alabama-Mississippi state line. The area was called Freedom Hills. As the labor pains of my mother grew more intense, the other children were sent walking down the gravel road to the house of an aunt and uncle about half a mile away. The four children could still hear the groans and chilling cries of their mother as she was giving birth. They were afraid and could only hope that it was going to be all right. The oldest child, thirteen-year-old Vera, held the hand of her five-year-old sister, Dorothy, as the boys, Buddy, age ten, and Johnny, age seven, walked down the road away from the house.

At 6:00 p.m., Lillie Mae Denton, who was thirty-four years old, gave birth to her sixth child with her husband, Dewey Denton, who was thirty-nine years old. Their first child, a baby girl, had been stillborn on January 3, 1924. With the kind help of a close friend and Dr. Finley, the old doctor who practiced medicine in Cherokee, the healthy baby boy was born. They named him Bobby Eugene.

It is said that only God's love for us exceeds a mother's love. However, only after we are older do we begin to really appreciate her love and all the things she did for us. We will never know the extent of her loving care and the sacrifices she endured to give birth to and raise us.

I can recall things from an early age, some of which occurred when I was less than two years old; I remember when my granddaddy died, and I was two then. My mother carried me down the path to his house wrapped in a blanket to see his body in the casket. Also, I remember as just a toddler walking down that pathway to my grandparents' house with my daddy. I held on to his finger as we walked, and it made me feel safe and loved. Is that not amazing to remember the details of an event at that age?

For the next several years, only flashbacks come into my mind—tiny episodes of my family life and the day-to-day things we did in those early years. As a child, one of my greatest fantasies was the constant wondering in my mind regarding what it would be like to be a grown-up man and have a wife and children of my own. Somehow, I could not imagine living to see that dream come true. Now, after all these years, God's plan for my life has made this fantasy become a reality. His plan for me has been greater than I could have ever wished for. He has given me a wonderful wife, three children, three grandchildren, and three great-grandchildren.

Chapter Two

Another big thing I remember well is World War II and the restrictions on buying some goods such as sugar, baking flour, coffee, tea, tires, and other things. I didn't understand why this was necessary. However, I thought I was really important as a child to have government stamps printed with my name on them. Of course, that's the way they distributed the rationing stamps to buy these short-supply commodities during the war. Every family member was allotted stamps to present to the store when the items were purchased. We only needed those few things because we raised almost everything we needed for food. Some clothing items were made from the material cooking flour was bagged in. My mother made my older sisters dresses when she had saved several flour bags. Most of the cloth bags had small designs on them and were two colors, like a white background with blue flowers.

Although my parents rarely attended church, they had strong family values. They always practiced the basic good things, like helping those who needed help and teaching us to respect others, especially older people. We never worked on Sundays; that was a day of rest.

In those days, parents loved their children differently than we do today. They gave the kids space and didn't hover over them every minute. As long as the parents knew where their children were, they let them play and imagine things in their minds and create things for themselves. It was a deep love but a tougher love. I know my mother and daddy would have killed or died for me if it were necessary. However, they never used the word love; they never did say to us, "I love you." But we knew they loved us. The unspoken love they gave their children was even more powerful. We never wondered whether our parents loved us. We knew they did, so that was all that mattered.

Discipline is a very important form of love. I can remember only a very few times I received what we now call a spanking; they were called whippings back then. The whippings I received were always with love and never once abusive. I can never remember verbal abuse being used against my siblings or me. We all were raised to respect our parents, and our parents respected us. However, there were times when a good whipping was just what the child needed. Children who receive discipline with love will love their parents more and become better people. The Holy Scripture even says, "Spare the rod and spoil the child" (Proverbs 13:24).

My granddaddy, John Amos Denton, who died when I was two years old, owned a large tract of land in Freedom Hills. He had many acres of woods and land along the creeks, where he raised cattle and sheep and worked a small farm. However, when he died, we only had the few acres for our home facilities. The remaining land was purchased by other family members. We didn't have good land to farm, so we farmed a tract of land owned by Mrs. Hamilton a mile down the road from our house. As a kid, I wondered why we were giving Mrs. Hamilton some of our cotton and corn. Never had I heard the term sharecropper. That's what we did with the little farm. We used Mrs. Hamilton's land and gave her a share of the crop that was produced.

Our family never thought that we may be poor or under-privileged in any way; most everyone we knew was like us. Sometimes, we found ourselves feeling sorry for a few families because they didn't have the things we had.

My daddy worked at the Reynolds aluminum plant in Muscle Shoals for a few years after World War II while we continued to maintain a small farming operation, along with having the usual vegetable gardens, a cow, pigs, and chickens. We also had three mules that were used for the farming work. We raised cotton and corn.

The cotton was sold, and the corn was used to feed the animals. We also took shelled corn to town and had it ground into cornmeal for bread (cornbread). Farm tractors were just beginning to be used by the small farmers as the war ended in the 1940s, but we never had one.

Bobby with Mom and Dad

My God and I

Chapter Three

Freedom Hills, comprised of thousands of acres of heavy woodland, got its name many years ago during the time of the illegal sale of alcohol. It was called Prohibition. This sparsely populated region of high hills, deep valleys, and clear streams of water was the perfect place to make a low-price spirit drink called moonshine or wildcat whiskey. Being caught making whiskey in those days was a prison offense, and many people served time for making the illegal beverage. The area was a great hideout for people who were running from the law trying to avoid going to jail; therefore, it was given the name Freedom Hills. I never was aware of any member of our family who made whiskey. However, we had several in the family who drank their share of it.

The area has the world's only Coon Dog Cemetery, and over the years it has become a well-known tourist attraction. Mr. Key Underwood, an avid coon hunter, buried his champion coon dog, Troop, in a special place near a road in 1936. The road was later named Coon Dog Road. A celebration with music and food is held at the cemetery every year. I was born three miles from the cemetery at my family's homestead. It's a very beautiful place.

As a child sitting on the front porch swing at our old house, I learned to love Freedom Hills. It was more than just a place to live; it was my home. I could hear the quietness of the hills around and the distant sounds of birds and animals who made their home there also.

At night, in the darkness, I would watch with amazement the millions of stars twinkling in the sky that God created and named them every one. I thought the amazing glow of the moon on clear nights was just beyond my fingertips, not dreaming it was about 240,000 miles above me. Nor did I realize that it was just a step away compared to the nearest star shining brightly in the sky, whose light takes four years to reach the earth traveling at 186,000 miles per second. I searched the sky to find the Big Dipper. I wonder if kids now know about the formation of stars making up what looks like a big dipper in the sky. We rarely see the stars now living in cities with all the lights.

I can't remember being taken to church or Sunday school as a child. My parents believed in God and were strict regarding respect, honesty, and good family values. However, there were times the family would go to one of the little churches around the area for a special gospel meeting or an all-day singing. I always looked forward to those events because they had lots of good food. The kids didn't stay inside the church building while the singing was going on; we played ball or explored the countryside.

After my parents became older, we moved to the small town of Cherokee seven miles away and attended the Baptist church. Without being exposed to regular church worship services as a child, somehow the family values teaching from my parents helped me grow up with the basic rules of the Bible. I thought telling the truth, being honest, and respecting others was what religion really was. Some people today who have never been taught the true Gospel of Jesus Christ feel the same way. They do not understand that just being a good person is all one must do to please God. We can never be good enough to be saved from our sins. Only the plan of salvation that God provided through His Son Jesus Christ can forgive our sins.

One of the most exciting times in my life was getting electricity in our house. While riding the school bus home every afternoon, I could see the construction advancing. There were no power tools, and all the holes for the poles were dug by hand with manual hole diggers. It was very time-consuming. Day after day, I would see the progress of getting the power lines built along the road to our house. In anticipation of having electricity, my daddy and a cousin wired the house and installed the things necessary to use electric power.

Days and weeks passed as I looked through the window of the school bus anticipating the day when the power would be turned on. I was flooded with an absolutely incredible feeling the day when I got off the school bus and ran into the house, turning on lights that were placed in the center of the ceiling in every room. The light was so bright! After using oil lamps all my life, it was fabulous. One has to experience what it is like living without electricity to fully appreciate having it.

Over the next year, our life changed a lot. The first new thing we got for the house was a refrigerator. Then came a washing machine, an electric radio, a cooking stove, and an electric iron. My mother was so happy to get these wonderful appliances after working so hard without them all her life.

By this time, my older sister, Vera had married. My brothers, Buddy and Johnny, soon followed. My sister Dorothy did the same within two years.

By this time, the farming was over, and only my mother and daddy and I were still there in the little house.

My God and I

Chapter Four

A turn in my life occurred when I was about nine years old. From the time he was a young man, my daddy had been musically inclined and could play the five-string banjo very well. I remember him talking about how he and a friend would ride a mule for long distances when they were young men to play music for square dances. He was also a champion buck dancer and continued to dance quite well until he reached almost ninety years old. He won blue ribbons several times at local festivals. As he became older, we often thought that the excessive exercise might be bad for him, but I suppose it proved to be good therapy; he lived to be ninety-two.

Once a lady who lived a few miles away borrowed his banjo to try and play it. In return, she let him keep an old guitar that she had. With the love for music already in my system, I began trying to play the old guitar. My daddy knew a few simple cords and taught them to me. I would strum and sing songs every day when I came home from school. After a few months, the lady's son brought the banjo back to us and was to pick up the guitar for his mother. I would have loved to keep the instrument, but I had no say in the matter.

The lady's son who came to our house to get the guitar was sweethearts with my cousin. He evidently wanted to impress her with his temper. They had a brief argument on the front porch as they were leaving our house. While showing off his mad spell, he held the guitar by its neck like holding a baseball bat and swung it hard, striking a post on the front porch and breaking the guitar into a thousand pieces. I could not believe it; he destroyed something I would have loved to have. Now it was gone.

To say the least, it was a bad thing that he had done and we didn't know what to do. There was nothing any of us could say. I was raised to forgive, but I can never forget what he did.

After that brief experience with the guitar, I could tell I was hooked on music and was more interested in listening to songs on the radio. I dreamed of someday becoming involved with music.

Over the next several weeks, another cousin, got a guitar that his parents had ordered for him from Sears and Roebuck, the big mail order company that published a catalogue with just about everything in it. I saw the guitar at his house one day while we were visiting his family. It looked just like new.

I asked about it, and my cousin's parents said their son never took any interest in playing it, and I could use it for a while. I couldn't wait to get home with it to play. It had a cord that allowed me to stand up and play, so I would stand up playing and singing like a big star. One day while performing for my mother, the cord holding the guitar broke and the guitar hit the hard floor with a bang. At first, I thought it was going to be fine and that no damage had been done; however, when I picked it up, I saw it was cracked from front to back. My next thought was that I was going to be in big trouble, but I was so glad my mother was there to see what had happened. When my dad came home from work, I was worried that he would be upset with me.

In my mind I thought, *I'm not having very much luck with using someone else's guitar.* My dad was calm and said we'd just have to tell my cousin's family what had happened and do what was right about it. A few days later, we carried the guitar over to my cousin's house about ten miles away. I was so sorry that this had happened and didn't know what the outcome would be.

When we got to their house I was shaking in my shoes. I just knew he would be mad at me. But when we showed him the crack and told him what happened, he said, "Well that's all right. You can just keep it." My heart almost jumped out of my chest.

Daddy later found someone to repair the crack with glue, and I enjoyed playing it for a long time.

Whenever we went visiting relatives and friends in the community, I always carried my guitar and was the entertainment. That guitar with the crack down its back was a treasure to me. I carried it to school on special days and would play and sing to the class.

Chapter Five

When I was twelve years old, I was considered to be the last child my parents would have. However, on February 15, 1950, my mother gave birth to a baby girl and they named her Cala Sue. My mother was forty-five and my dad was fifty. Some family members worried whether they would be able to care for her as they grew older. As it turned out, Cala was the best thing that ever happened to my parents. She was so sweet and smart and lovable. In school she was a straight A student and a cheerleader for the high school sports program.

In the meantime, my little music career continued to develop and opportunities came along often. At the age of fourteen, I teamed up with two older boys, Julian Henry and his brother Bobby, who could play music extremely well. They lived several miles from me across Freedom Hills and had a car so they came to our house often to play music. Almost every session would include a tune or two from Daddy on his banjo. Soon, another friend Bob Rogers, who played the big bass fiddle joined us.

When I was fifteen, our little group was playing on local radio stations in the Muscle Shoals area, and we'd established ourselves as up-and-coming young entertainers.

Later, we were invited to come to Nashville to perform on the WSM radio program called the *Junior Grand Ole Opry* and compete for a guest spot on the real *Grand Ole Opry* along with other prizes. When the big day came, we all loaded into their 1949 Ford car with the big bass fettle inside the car with us and headed for Nashville before daybreak.

We did the radio program that Saturday, along with a few other contestants, and drove the long 150 miles back home. It was a big deal and a dream come true for me. Singing on one of the most popular and powerful radio stations in the country was breathtaking. We had to wait a week to learn who would be advanced to the semifinal competition.

The next Saturday, with my ear glued to the radio, I could not believe it when I heard the announcer say, "This week's winner is Bobby Denton and his band from Cherokee, Alabama." This meant that the next week we would go back to Nashville to compete for the final prize. By this time, the whole area of Northwest Alabama was pulling for us to win the finals.

The second trip to the Music City was even more exciting, and we sang and played on the program with the confidence of winning. The next week was long, as I waited for the results to learn who the winner would be. It was heartbreaking to learn that a girl from Kentucky was the top winner, and we were runner-up. The group continued to perform around the area and doing radio programs.

The little band entered the big talent show at the Mid-South Fair in Memphis and won first place, the blue ribbon. This gave me and the others popularity and opened many new doors for us in the future.

After discussing the possibility of moving from the little house where I was born, my parents made the decision to move into town. There seemed to be no reason to live in the house seven miles from town any more. The family was gone, building their own lives; my little sister, Cala, and I were the only kids remaining at home. So, we rented a house in Cherokee and moved in. The house wasn't as modern as most, but it was better than our house in the country. It really was a big change for us, but we soon became accustomed to being closer to stores and the schools. It was nice to be able to walk downtown in just a few minutes.

One could buy almost everything for everyday use in Cherokee. It had a post office, a drugstore, a barber shop, and three general merchandise stores. General merchandise stores were like super-small Walmarts, selling everything from groceries to clothing and hardware. For a larger variety of things, the people there would drive or ride a bus to what we called uptown, which was the tri-cities of Tuscumbia, Sheffield, and Florence. Muscle Shoals was in place but just beginning to develop from its incorporation in 1923.

Most of the land in Muscle Shoals was owned by out-of-state property speculators who believed that Henry Ford would purchase the newly constructed Wilson Dam on the nearby Tennessee River. The giant dam was built as part of President Roosevelt's New Deal plan to restore the economy after the Great Depression.

The dam was a masterpiece of modern construction and served as a flood control and river navigational system. Wilson Dam could also produce massive amounts of electricity at a very low cost. Henry Ford's plan was to purchase the dam and use the abundant electric power to operate the auto plant he was planning to build near Muscle Shoals. If the US Congress had not blocked the sale of the dam to Henry Ford, the huge auto plant at Detroit, Michigan, would have been built just east of Muscle Shoals. The area is now called "Ford City."

After all those years, there are sidewalks, fire hydrants, and other infrastructure in the city of Muscle Shoals that were put in place in anticipation of the Ford Motor Company development. Also, almost every street in Muscle Shoals has a sister street by the same name in Detroit.

After moving to town, I had a wider variety of new friends to associate with. I found that my interests began to change as I spent more time with friends and hanging out in town.

My schoolwork was of no interest to me. I never thought education would be anything I would need. All I wanted was to be an entertainer someday. My time at home with my parents and little sister was just not exciting enough for me. We didn't have a television or telephone, and there was no incentive for my imagination to amuse me as it had while we were living in the isolation of the country house.

As time went by, I made a special friend through my association with music who lived in Florence. Tom Stafford was a few years older and worked at the Shoals Theater in Florence as assistant manager. Tom's dad owned and operated the City Drug Store just down the street from the theater. Since I was only fifteen and didn't have a car, most of the trips I made to Florence on weekends to visit with Tom consisted of hitchhiking a ride.

I would stand out on the side of Highway 72 in Cherokee with my guitar and catch a ride. Everybody who didn't have a car did that in those days. I never dreamed that it may be dangerous. Tom loved music and was a good short story writer and songwriter. Although he was somewhat eccentric, he was a good person. He and I would collaborate on writing songs and dreamed of being successful in the music business someday.

We worked together well and were the catalyst for the development of the famous recording studio upstairs over the City Drug Store. The recording studio was the beginning point for several young musicians who later made it very big in music.

The downside of coming to Florence and working with Tom was all the time I spent waiting for him to get off work at the theater. But that waiting time became a blessing to me later.

When I came to Florence, I spent nights at my older brother Buddy's house in Sheffield. He had been drafted into the army, and his wife Lorene, and her mother lived just across the river in Sheffield.

My brother's house was located next door to a very nice couple who had two girls. They were kind, loving people, who never met a person they didn't like. I had noticed the daughters; Barbara was thirteen, and Carolyn who was eight. They always said hi to me when I came to my brother's house. Barbara was a little reserved, and Carolyn was spirited and very animated.

When one is fifteen years old, one tends to think the person who is two years younger is too much of a kid to think beyond, "Hi, how are you?"

In school, there were a couple of girls who I would have liked to have been sweethearts with, but they never seemed to want me as a boyfriend. I had never been on a date and knew almost nothing about the "birds and bees."

Barbara became prettier and nicer almost every time I would see her. I realize that God's plan for me was beginning to take shape in this new time of my life, but I never thought much about spiritual matters at that age.

Chapter Six

After Barbara and I had met several times, we became at ease talking with each other in the yard when I was at my brother's house. Her little sister, Carolyn, was always there and talking more than Barbara. One weekend, while I was waiting for Tom to get off work, I decided not to waste my time sitting in the movie, so I went across the street to a drugstore that had privet telephone booths and called Barbara's house. Back then, the phones were not the dial type; you had to give the number you were calling to a live operator. I found an empty phone booth, picked up the receiver, and inserted a dime to make the call.

The operator said, "Number please."

I said, "3456J please."

Luckily, Barbara answered the phone.

I was relieved that I didn't have to ask one of her parents if I could speak with her. She was nice to talk with, and we enjoyed our conversations. Sometimes we would talk for a long time, and the calls to Barbara became an important part of my weekend visits to the tri-cities. I believe that her parents only allowed her to talk to me because they trusted me as their neighbor's brother. The phone calls continued for about a year, becoming longer and longer.

At times, Barbara and I would sit on the front porch swinging and talking but very seldom in private because Carolyn was always around. She didn't want to miss a thing, though we would have loved for her to go inside the house and leave us alone.

My music continued to be my main interest, along with always having a job around town. My daddy purchased a new power lawn mower to cut our grass at home, and I used it to mow lawns all around town. People would pay me from two dollars to five dollars to cut their grass depending on the size of their yard. I always had a side job doing about anything that needed to be done. The money was used as my spending money for visits to the drugstore soda fountain and for trips on the weekends to play music.

My friends and I never did anything really bad, except smoke cigarettes when we could afford them. A pack of cigarettes was twenty cents a pack. I can remember when they went up to twenty-one cents and a Coke went up from a nickel to six cents. The drink companies installed a little box on the side of the machine to put the penny in.

The most fun thing we boys did was playing football after school. In the 1950s, our school at Cherokee had a very good football team. My time playing football in High School only lasted a couple of years because I was only interested in playing music. I always played defensive linebacker against the first-team players as they practiced. As the second-string center, I didn't get a lot of real game playing time unless the score was a runaway in Cherokee's favor.

In the early 1950s, we got a new movie theater in Cherokee. The old theater was not very nice. It had wooden bench seats that got higher at each row toward the back, so if one sat in the back, it was high off of the floor. So, the new one with real seats was a great change for us.

The day I became sixteen, I got my driver's license. I'd thought that time would never come. Since my brother was in the army, my sister-in-law was easy to persuade and allowed me to drive their car for special trips around town. Driving meant I could have a date if Barbara's parents would let her go with me and I could use my sister-in-law's new car.

At this time, Barbara was only fourteen and, and like me, she had never been on a date. We didn't have the nerve to ask if we could go out together for a long time, but the special event finally came for us to go on a double date with friends.

In a few weeks, Barbara's parents reluctantly agreed to let her go with me to a movie only if we promised not to go to a drive-in theater. Of course, we said that we would not. For our first date alone, I walked over from my brother's house next door and chatted for a few minutes with her parents, during which I was reminded to be careful and to be back before ten o'clock.

Barbara and I got in the car and were driving away when we heard something in the back seat. That's right, it was Carolyn, snickering like a nosy eight-year-old stowaway. We laughed it off and carried her back home to receive a good talking to by her mother and dad.

That first date was scary for us. I had not ever kissed a girl before, and I doubted if Barbara had ever kissed a boy. But it didn't take me very long to find out that she was a dynamite kisser. During the next couple of years, we went out together on Saturday nights if I was not playing music somewhere.

In those days, there was almost nothing to do other than go to the movie and later stop by the drive-in for a curb service drink and hamburger.

Ours was the generation that invented going "parking." Couples would go to a secluded place to park the car and smooch. I don't know if kids ever do that anymore, as we can see them out in public view doing more than we did while parking in our days.

Our relationship became serious fairly quickly, and we realized that we may be destined to be together throughout our lives. Kids did that a lot back then and called it "going steady." Most young people never dated more than one person before marriage. It's amazing how well that system worked.

Couples like this very rarely divorced when they did become married. That's the way our parents raised us. Marriage was a one man, one woman, for life institution. These values were set into all of our minds as we grew up, and I'm glad they were; it's biblical teaching.

My years in high school were filled with exciting events. I did everything but study my books. Most of the girls had boyfriends, some of them were older boys, so they never thought of me as anyone other than a close friend. They all knew that I had a girlfriend in Sheffield, although they had never met her. It turned out to be a good thing that Barbara and I lived in different towns because there is an old saying "absence makes the heart grow fonder," and I believe it's true.

I continued to always have jobs around the community, from chopping and picking cotton, to about anything else. One winter, I had the job of going to the Baptist church early on Sunday mornings and building fires in coal-burning stoves that were used for heating the building. The church paid me five dollars a week, and I thought that was a good deal.

I had already begun attending church there and found it was a good place to socialize. Later, my parents and little sister began to attend the services on Sunday also. My older sister and her husband attended the Methodist church, and some of my cousins attended the Church of Christ. I often wondered, *Why does everybody need to go to a different church?* It was a very good question, but I never had the nerve to ask about it.

During those early years as a teenager, I had a strong inner feeling that God was directing my life. Somehow, I was just aware of my vulnerability as a young person and wanted to do the right thing. There's a saying, "Always do the right thing, and you know what that is." That is a profound statement, but I didn't fully understand its meaning back then.

My God and I

Chapter Seven

I suppose everyone has a special person in life that can be identify as having the greatest influence on us. When I think about that person in my life, I don't need to give it a second thought. It is Willodine Malone, one of my teachers from elementary school and later through high school. Her adult friends called her Billie, and she was loved by every person who knew her.

Mrs. Malone, as we all called her, had a certain love that was very encouraging and would make you want to learn. Her teachings went far beyond the regular academics and the appreciation for the arts. She taught me values that continue to influence my life today. I love Mrs. Malone as a person who played a major role in shaping my life. It was an honor to be asked to sing at her funeral.

She encouraged me to stay in school when I became disenchanted and wanted to join the US Marines. I had already picked up the enlistment papers that had to be signed by my parents because I was only seventeen years old. The final decision was made when I carried the papers to my daddy, and he said, "Boy, you better keep yourself in school. I'm not going to sign this paper."

Thank goodness for that advice and firm parenting. If he had signed the papers, it would have destroyed my life and all the plans I had made for myself through the years.

However, just to save face, I did join the Alabama National Guard with his permission. A few other friends joined up with me and it made us feel real grown-up.

However, it was not too long until I began thinking about the National Guard in the same way as I did about school. I didn't like it, and it was getting in the way of my music life. I managed to muddle through the three-year enlistment only to find out that it included another five-year stint in the US Army Reserve. This was a killer for me to endure because, by the time the enlistment was up, I would be out of high school, have ventured deeply into a musical career, have gotten married, and have fathered two children.

At one time in the early 60s, the 491st MP unit of which I was a member was on standby alert with orders to the coast of Cuba. That time was scary for the whole country. And, thank God, it worked out regarding the placement of Soviet missiles in Cuba just ninety miles off the US shore

My junior and senior years in high school were filled with new adventures. I was active, going to every school event and entering talent shows around the region. Through my association with Tom Stafford, I had established a wider circle of friends in the area of music and radio. This was about the time that Florence's native Sam Phillips discovered Elvis Presley.

One Saturday morning, I was finishing up a radio program with my band at WLAY in Muscle Shoals. As I walked out the door of the studio, I noticed three young men standing in the lobby. I spoke to them as if I were a big radio star and they were a wannabe group. I walked over to them. "Hello, I'm Bobby Denton," I said.

The good-looking one with the black hair said, "Hi, Bobby. I'm Elvis Presley."

That name didn't ring a bell with me, so I said hello to the other two fellows, Scotty Moore and Bill Black, who became famous as backup players for Elvis.

Later in the day, I realized the three of them were in town to perform at the Sheffield Community Center with a group of big country music stars. A couple of my friends and I went to the show just to see the *Grand Ole Opry* stars and never gave a thought about going to see Elvis; we had never heard of him. Little did we know that Sam Phillips, who had started a small record company in Memphis, had booked Elvis on the show as a warm-up act for the big stars and to test the market for his newfound talent.

The building was packed because we very seldom had big-name entertainers come to the area. The audience never suspected that this show in Sheffield, Alabama, would go down in history as the big break for Elvis Presley on his way to becoming the King of Rock and Roll.

When Elvis, Scotty, and Bill were introduced he began singing "That's All Right, Mama;" I had never heard a sound like it. I said to myself, *What is this?* With Elvis playing his acoustic guitar, Scotty playing his simple licks on the electric guitar, and Bill playing the stand-up bass, it was awesome! It was not country, and it was not blues; all I knew was that it was different, and I loved it. By the time Elvis had finished his first song, the crowd was tearing the house down, and he sang the song again.

Then after the audience got under control, he did the flip side of his new Sun record, "Blue Moon of Kentucky," an old

Bill Monroe bluegrass song. But he didn't do it like Bill Monroe at all. It was a killer. It was so different, and it was actually what the young people at that point in time wanted to hear. We wanted something different from the music that was the mainstream country and pop, and Sam Phillips had found it. It was said after the program was over that one of the big stars told the booking agent, "Don't ever book me with this guy Elvis again!"

The next day after the show, all the local radio stations were playing the Elvis Presley record. Elvis had already had some success in Memphis, but we had never been exposed to his music in our area. Day by day, the momentum built for him, and within weeks, his popularity had spread around the country.

Within a year after the Sheffield show, Sun Records put on another show in Sheffield. And this time, Elvis and his band were driving a new pink Cadillac. The previous time he had been to the area—when I'd spoken with him at the radio station—he had been driving a 1953 Chevrolet. This latest trip to Sheffield, arranged by Sam Phillips and his brother Jud Phillips, a mastermind promoter, included the complete Sun Records gold mine of recording artists.

It was a big deal and became known as the debut of several new stars. Johnny Cash was part of the group, along with Carl Perkins, the singer of the hit "Blue Suede Shoes." Carl was about to hit the top with his record when he had an automobile accident that almost took his life. The accident kept him from becoming a big superstar at that time. However, he managed to make a comeback within a few years. Elvis later recorded "Blue Suede Shoes," and most people never knew that Carl Perkins had the original record, which I personally think was better than the Elvis version.

With all these new talents being recorded and promoted by Sun Records, I thought that I may have a chance to be one of the people recorded by the up-and-coming company. So, one of my friends and I drove to Memphis one day hoping to meet Sam Phillips and maybe audition for him.

After driving to Memphis, all we got to see was the famous studio where all the new recording artists had made their records. It was not overly impressive, just one big room with a control room adjacent to it and a large glass window overlooking the studio. Most radio stations had studios as nice, but it served the purpose it was intended to serve, and I felt humbled by having visited the historic place for a few minutes.

Sam was out of town, and he never called me back. I was deeply disappointed but felt somewhat like the young salesman who knocked on his first door while hoping no one was at home. After Sam Phillips had discovered Elvis, he launched more artists who became famous, including Charlie Rich and Roy Orbison.

Later, there was talk that Sun Records was preparing to come out with another new artist with blond, curly hair, and a few people around home just knew it was going to be me. It was Jerry Lee Lewis, who rocked the world with the songs *"Whole Lot of Shaking Going On"* and *"Great Balls of Fire."*

Jerry Lee became a star fast and had several hit records; however, his rough lifestyle and his marriage to his very young cousin almost destroyed his career. The story broke while he was touring in Europe, and the fans rebelled against him and boycotted his shows. Fans in the United States were about as defiant, and his popularity plummeted.

Chapter Eight

Meanwhile, I was going into my senior year at school and having fun doing everything. The last year in high school was my happiest of all. One day in January 1957, I was called to the principal's office to receive a phone call. I had no idea who could be calling me at school. I got to the phone excited and out of breath. The caller was James Joiner in Florence. He asked me if I would be interested in coming to see him and talk about recording a record for his new recording company.

I said, "Absolutely."

We agreed that I would meet with him on Saturday. So, on Saturday I hitched a ride to Florence to meet with him. He asked me a lot of questions about my plans when I finished school and if I would like to record the first record for the new company he and a few others were forming. This was a dream come true for me, so without question I said yes. It was almost unbelievable to think about me actually making a record that would be played on the radio and sold in record stores.

Mr. Joiner went on to say he had written some songs, and one of them, "A Fallen Star," may be good for my record. He sang the song to me, and he asked what I thought.

I immediately said, "It's great. I would love to record it."

But after thinking about it later, I thought to myself, What did he think an eighteen-year-old kid would say? I would have said I loved it regardless of whether the song was good or not good.

So, plans were quickly made to record the song with another of Joiner's songs called "Carla," which I truly didn't like at all. But he never knew how I felt about the song.

The next thing the baby recording company Tune Records had to decide was where the songs would be recorded. The only professional recording studios in existence were in Memphis and Nashville, and they were used by the big recording companies. Mr. Joiner decided to record it locally at the only studio and tape recorder in the area that might do an acceptable job. That was at the radio station WLAY, where I had met Elvis earlier. Even with the good studio and recorder, the setup and conditions were very primitive for recording a record to be released for radio play and retail sales.

The recording session was done in about an hour or two using three musical instruments and a local gospel quartet for backup. Of course, we didn't have the equipment to overdub mistakes. Every instrument and the vocal part had to be performed correctly throughout the entire song. There was no altering parts of the recording at a later time. Everything had to be done right at the same time. Also, the engineer who was the radio station disc jockey had to do his work and carry on the regular programming of the station at the same time.

When the session was over, I was so proud to have had this great experience. However, I think all of us would have tried to do a better job had we known we were making history. We had just finished making the first master record ever recorded and distributed in the state of Alabama.

The class of '57 continued to have fun enjoying our final year in school together with dreams and anticipations for the future. There was almost no talk among the class members about going to college. The way we were raised, we thought getting a high school diploma would be about all we would ever need. It was easy to get a job around the area with all the large industrial plants. These jobs meant having a good income with retirement and medical insurance for all employees, allowing them to have a much better way of life than their parents as they raised a family. We had never thought beyond having a new car and a nice house.

My God and I

Chapter Nine

In a week, the records were received from the record pressing company in Nashville and a copy was sent to radio stations all over the region, including the Birmingham area. The kids at school thought I was really something, especially the young girls; they were my biggest fans. The radio stations began playing the song, *"A Fallen Star,"* and it was selling in local record shops. I was thrilled and could not believe what was happening to me. Could it be that I was going to be what I had always wanted to be in life? I was happy, and everyone loved me as a friend because I was just Bobby to them

Then in just two weeks after my record was released, I learned that a big-name artist had recorded my song, and his record was recorded in Nashville with a major record company. When I heard that, by heart almost broke. The song was recorded by Grand Ole Opry star Jimmy Newman. Within days, more covers of the song were released by popular singers Ferlin Husky, Jim Reeves, and The Hill Toppers, who were also with major label companies. I couldn't believe that my simple little record was being overshadowed by all these other people who were being pushed by big record companies.

I didn't let the situation regarding the record trouble me too much. I still had lots of things going on, and Tune Records was making plans for me to record my second record at an old empty movie house in Sheffield, the Ritz Theater. It was only a shell of a building with all the seating removed.

Bobby recording at the Ritz

The place was not the norm for a recording studio but by then technology had improved greatly and I was confident the new record would turn out better than the last one. The studio had more modern equipment, but we still had to record as before, doing the song in one take. With the large area of the old theater, every instrument was located in different areas of the floor space and used a separate microphone. That was something we didn't have for the first record at the radio station.

Finally, Friday evening, May 31 at 7:30 p.m. came, and the fifty-four members of the class of 1957 received our diploma. I had never felt so happy. I could feel the love of my classmates and teachers. I could feel the love of my parents and members of my family. And I could feel the love of Barbara, who attended the graduation and by now was a constant flame in my heart. It was a feeling of happiness and sadness at the same time.

A sudden independence came over me that also brought to my mind that I was now grown up with responsibilities.

I hit the ground running with my music every day. The band consisted of Earl "Peanut" Montgomery playing the electric guitar, Eddie Goodwin playing the drums, and Ray Barger playing the stand-up bass. Our little group had a great time doing what we loved. I was like the daddy of the group of boys because I was just about to turn nineteen years old.

My first car after graduation was a 1953 Plymouth four-door. The car would hardly hold the four of us with all the instruments. Ray's bass fiddle was in a canvas cover on top of the car. Eddie's drums and Peanut's amp were in the trunk. This meant that mine and Peanut's guitars were inside the car with us. This worked out well for trips around the area, but the trips to Birmingham were long and cramped for us. We played lots of times on Saturdays in Birmingham on the radio station WVOK and at new car dealerships, as well as a big Saturday night dance at the National Guard Armory.

The '53 Plymouth was just too small for us to travel in. So I went shopping around Birmingham for a big, four-door Cadillac with air-conditioning and all the extras. After finding one, I made a tentative deal to trade for it, but there was one problem; I didn't have any money or credit. So when I got home, I asked my brother Buddy if he would help me buy the car. Wanting to help me, he went with me to the bank and co-signed for the money to trade for the car.

It was a 1954 Cadillac Fleetwood, and the color was lavender. The payments at the bank were forty-eight dollars per month. At that time, gas was about twenty-five cents a gallon. However, it was hard to realize much of a profit after paying the other boys a piddling amount and having money for food and clothing. But that car looked like a million dollars with the bass strapped on the top. It was just like the big stars in the music business.

As the months went by, and the road became longer, I

found myself always away from home and had very little time to see Barbara.

When one is nineteen years old, it seems like time is dragging, and I was anxious to do more in the area of music. At one point, RCA Records wanted to buy my contract from Tune, but Tune didn't want to sell. This was crushing to me because, if I had gone with RCA, my career would have been different; I would have been with a giant company rather than the little local company with very small distribution and no funds to promote me. I felt trapped, and my dreams of becoming a star were dwindling.

I was in love with Barbara and knew I had to make a choice. I didn't know what the future held for me; I hadn't made plans for a career other than music to make a living. I was worried that Barbara would get tired waiting for me, and we may not continue our plans together. We had already talked about being married some day when she finished high school. I was afraid and confused, and I knew down deep inside that it was not going to work out. It was clear to me that I would not be able to do the music and work at another job at the same time. I had to decide which way I intended to go with my life.

The last performance we made was in Rome, Georgia, about two hundred miles from home. Knowing this would be the last show for us was sad. I gave it a lot of thought and decided to quit music and liquidate my assets in the business. First, I told Peanut, Eddie, and Ray that I was quitting and wished them all well. Next, I told Barbara and, at the same time, asked if she would marry me. The only material assets I had were the car and my guitar, and I owed more on the car than it was worth.

A friend of mine who ran the used car lot where I had bought the Plymouth tried to sell it for me with no luck. He finally carried it to a used car auction out of town and sold it to the highest bidder. The value of a used Cadillac that was previously owned by a small-time rock and roll singer was not good. The car sold at a ridiculously low price, so I had to refinance the balance on monthly payments.

I sold my D-28 Martin guitar back to Forbes Piano Company for about half the price I had paid for it. That guitar would be worth thousands of dollars today.

The boys in the band continued to play music and they were quickly drafted by other bands in the area. Most boys who played music with the bands in the area went on to be professional musicians and are part of the famous recording industry that later developed in Muscle Shoals.

Bobby and Barbara

As for me, the biggest thing I had to do was swallow my pride and get a real job to make a living.

It was a big drop from being well known in the area for most of my life and becoming somewhat successful with music to a forty-dollar-a-week job with a termite company. Perhaps the hardest fall was from driving a Cadillac down to driving a 1946 Ford. At first, I thought my life was over, and I didn't have the courage to be in public with the shame I felt. I had always worked hard when I was growing up, but work was not what I had planned to do for a living.

The Band

Chapter Ten

Later, I managed to get better jobs, and my life began settling down. I started to realize that I would have to work at a real job for the rest of my life. I tried to be content; to do as most of my school friends were doing; and to live the way I had been taught—get a job, get married, and have a family.

So, on November 22, 1957, Barbara and I were married at her parents' house with only our family in attendance. It was a simple service, with cake and punch, and then we were on our way for a weekend honeymoon.

Barbara was seventeen, and I was nineteen. We had already rented an upstairs apartment and were excited about starting our new lives together. We later moved to a house, which was much better given we didn't have to climb stairs. Barbara spent her days fixing up inside the house, and I was becoming more adapted to working in a manufacturing plant.

After only four months of marriage, Barbara became pregnant. This was a shocker that we didn't need at that time. With no medical insurance and little money, we were afraid for our uncertain future. I was beginning to adjust to life without being involved with music. However, my mind continued to flash thoughts of what I may have accomplished in music.

And then one day, without any prior warning, I received a call from the new owner of radio station WLAY, who said he and another associate would like to come to my house and talk with me. Of course, I said yes, and the meeting time was set. I had no idea what this was all about.

They came to our house and began talking to me about plans they had for a new record company and what they wanted to offer me. It seemed their plan was very well thought out and could be a great success. They told me a new record company was being formed by them, two doctors, along with the legendary promoter Judd Phillips. The company would be called Judd Records. They wanted me to be their first project and even had a song selected to be on the first record. The story went on and on, and they said I would be featured on the popular *Dick Clark Saturday Night Show* on ABC television from New York.

By now, my head was spinning, and I could not believe what they were offering me. They already had the appearance booked on the TV program and plans to record the song. Judd Phillips was a master promoter and was known throughout the nation by record distributors as well as by radio and TV contacts. Judd had a good track record for his talent in promoting artists, from Elvis to several others who his brother Sam had recorded on Sun Records. This proposal was, by far, the biggest opportunity that anyone could ever imagine. It was hard to believe that I was their choice for this chance of a lifetime.

My problem was I had already quit music and I was married. Besides that, we were expecting a baby in a few months.

I had never heard of an opportunity like I was being offered. They were planning to record me in Nashville at the famous Owen Bradley Studio, with the best musicians in the business.

I knew Barbara was not excited about me getting back into music. I could see it on her face. I knew she must have been thinking, *Well, here we go again—Bobby gone and, even worse, this time I'm home alone and pregnant.*

I could understand that, and I was tempted to just say no thanks and not take the out-of-this world opportunity.

Every questionable scenario as to why I couldn't do it was countered by the reply, "We will do it," or, "That's all right; we'll take care of it." They said that Barbara could go to Nashville with me to make the record and go with me to New York for the TV program.

When she said, "I'm beginning to show, and I don't have the proper clothes to wear," they said, "We will buy you a complete new wardrobe."

Then we wondered about my job and how we could continue to pay our bills. They said, "We will pay your salary from the time you leave your job, until you start making the big money later on."

It seemed that there was nothing we could say to discourage their determination to have me do this project. The conversation went on for hours, so we decided to think about it and meet again the next day.

At the second meeting, more of the details were revealed and questions asked. They had plans for a record promotional tour after the TV show that would last about six weeks, covering every major city from the entire East Coast west through Oklahoma. They had a customized bus complete with every amenity, including a phone, restroom, and sleeping accommodations. The plans also stipulated that I would appear on the TV program in early September, on the first weekend of the new school year. The set was already planned for the new song *"Back to School"* that I was to perform.

After doing the TV program, Barbara would be flying home while I continued on the tour. Never in my wildest dreams could I have imagined a chance such as this. I was in shock and spellbound, but I could see Barbara was not convinced this would be good for her. However, I believe she also knew this was a very big deal, and if she stood in my way, it could affect our marriage later. Both of us knew this was a chance of a lifetime, and it was just too good to pass up. So, we said yes to the proposal made by the company.

The next thing I had to do was give my notice to my employer that I would be quitting the job in two weeks. In the meantime, a date was set for the song to be recorded in Nashville.

Judd Records had asked Buddy Killen, a Florence native who was the vice president of Tree Publishing Company, to produce the session and arrange for the players and background voices. At this point, they didn't have the B-side song selected for the record. So when we arrived in Nashville on the day of the session, we went to Buddy Killen's office to select another song.

Tree Publishing had skyrocketed over the last year with big hit songs like *"Heartbreak Hotel"* by Elvis. We previewed several songs, trying to find anything that would work out for the other side of *"Back to School,"* which they thought would be the hit song after I had sung it on the *Dick Clark Show*.

After hearing several demos, Buddy said, "See what you think about this song, '*Sweet and Innocent*,' written by Rick Hall and Billy Sherrill from Hamilton, Alabama. He played the simple demo for us.

"That's it," I said. "I think that is a good tune. Let's do it."

And so, Buddy put his creative mind in action and began imagining what he wanted the two songs to sound like and who he wanted to play the music. It was like a miracle that he hired the very best people in Nashville to play on the record. They were all right there in town and available to play. Buddy Killen knew his way around the music business and was one of the brightest music people I have ever known.

Every person who played on that session was the best in Nashville. The nice fellow who got me a Coke during the session was the music legend Boots Randolph who played the saxophone. The quiet, clean-cut fellow who played the piano was Floyd Cramer, who later became popular around the world with his song "*Last Date.*" The background voices were the Jordanaires, who became famous performing with Elvis Presley, and a girl singer, Anita Kerr, who headed up the very popular Anita Kerr Singers.

The Owen Bradley studio was more advanced than the studios we had used before and was considered the best in the business. Everyone was happy with the results of the new recording. The technology allowing track recording was just coming to the Nashville studio, but we still recorded with everyone in the same room as we had done in the makeshift studios in Muscle Shoals.

After the recording session was over, Barbara and I rode back home with two co-owners of Judd Records, Dr. Robert

Maxwell and Dr. Alvin McClendon. I was so happy with the recording session. It was the best record by far that I had ever made. I loved both sides of it and could hardly wait for the release date.

There were still lots of things to do. We went shopping in Memphis and purchased Barbara several new outfits to wear to New York and afterward while she was expecting the baby. All the people at work were excited about me going to New York and being on national television. As the September 6 date came nearer, Barbara and I were growing more anxious about leaving and saying goodbye to our family and friends.

The local newspaper was running articles about the coming event, and the people of the Muscle Shoals area were waiting to see their local boy on network television. We left on the bus on Thursday and traveled all that day and the next night. Upon arrival in New York, at the Manhattan Hotel, we must have looked like a group of bums after traveling all that distance, and Barbara was showing greatly by then. But it was fine because we didn't see a single person we knew.

The group of us checked into the hotel and were assigned our rooms. Making the trip with us on the bus was Judd Phillips; Dr. McClendon; and James Phifer, a nice black fellow who became my best friend over the next several weeks. James looked out for me and made sure my clothes were clean. He also served as an assistant for everyone on the six-week tour that followed the TV show.

We rested during the day because I had my first meeting with the TV producers and Dick Clark later that afternoon at the ABC studio, three blocks away on 44th Street. After taking a taxi to the studio, I went inside, and all the guest who were to appear on the program were seated waiting for instructions and to meet Dick Clark. When Dick came in, he welcomed us and asked that we stand as the producer called our names.

When my name was called and I stood up, Dick Clark commented, "Oh good, a teenager."

Next, we were instructed as to what format the show would have and what we should know about being on a big TV program. First, the producer said that this program was sponsored by Beechnut Gum and was the most watched TV program in the nation that year. He said that forty-four million people would be watching. The viewing audience was that large because there were only three major networks on TV at that time.

After the briefing, a man said I would have to join the TV and Movie Actors Union before the performance and to be on other major TV stations around the country. So, the record company paid my dues of $120. The minimum union pay for the appearance was $155.

The next day, we had two rough rehearsals and a tweaking of the program timing. This was September 6, 1958. Everything on TV then was live; videotape would come along later. A few of the big shows had already begun to film programs, but ABC had not begun doing that on this program yet. They even rehearsed the commercials and camera shots. They had had a special-made set just for me.

In late afternoon, before the live program was to air, we had a dress and camera rehearsal with a live audience. I wore a plaid shirt with blue jeans and white buck shoes. And I had to go upstairs to have the makeup person give me the usual nonglare facial treatment, which is standard for TV. Then that audience was replaced by all new people who were waiting outside to see the show.

Barbara came to the dress rehearsal and afterward went back to the hotel to see the program on TV. The program came off without a glitch, and I was so proud of myself and for the opportunity to have this experience.

Chapter Eleven

By the time the TV program was over, I had begun to know the other entertainers who performed with me and quickly realized I was in extremely prestigious company. Among the stars appearing on the program were the famous Ruth Brown and the great singer Tommy Edwards. Edwards sang "It's all in the Game," which later became a top seller around the country. At that time in the late 50s, with rock and roll music on the rise, the radio airwaves were saturated with new groups of performers who could shoot to the top of the charts in a matter of weeks through the relatively new medium of television and the even more popular radio.

One of the most memorable things that occurred at the event came as we were leaving the TV studio. The studio was located on 44th Street and just off Broadway, near Times Square. The location was in the same vicinity of several off-Broadway theatres. The pedestrian traffic was so crowded the police department closed off 44th street to automobile traffic when the theaters were active. They even notified us at the program briefing that we would need our own security. The police were on foot and horseback to manage the crowds of people.

As we exited a side door of the TV studio, I saw the street completely packed with people and teenagers screaming as we made our way onto the sidewalk. I had never seen anything like it. Besides the people who had filled the TV studio and were waiting outside to see us coming out, there was a play ending just across the street from the door we were exiting. The street was jammed with yelling kids and excited fans pressing against each other.

Then I heard some guy shout loud from across the street standing on a fireplug. He yelled, "Who is it?"

The young girls around me shouted back, "It's Bobby Denton," to which the man replied, "I've never heard of him."

That was a big deal being in New York City and fans surrounding me like that; it was almost unbelievable.

As I was making my way through all the people, I wondered to myself, "Where in the world is James? He's supposed to be here with me." Then I looked back and saw James signing autographs for the kids. They didn't know who was who; they just knew we were all coming out of the TV studio. Finally, we made it down the street to the Manhattan Hotel with a feeling of success that I had never experienced before.

Our entire group from home who'd come to New York to support me on the program was waiting at the hotel with Barbara to congratulate me for the good job they said I had done. Everyone felt the new record would do well for us. Later, we all went to the famous restaurant Sardi's, for dinner and I could not believe the bill's total was $120 for the group. It would be $1,000 or more today.

The next day, Barbara and three of the record company owners, with their wives, flew back to Muscle Shoals. It was sad seeing them leave me alone in the largest city in the country. Barbara had never flown before, and I was worried about how she would make the trip. With them gone, that left only Judd Phillips, Dr. McClendon, James, and the bus driver to finish the long tour with me.

After the TV program, the New York radio stations began playing my record and the area record distributor ordered seventy thousand copies. We continued around the city for a couple of days to meet big-name disc jockeys. I wanted to do some sightseeing while we were there, so James and I walked around Manhattan, up and down Broadway, to see everything. I had never dreamed of a twenty-four-hour-a-day city, but that's what it was, with people going and coming around the clock.

While walking along Broadway, we passed a shoe shine stand sitting back in a little area at the edge of the sidewalk. So, James and I decided to get our shoes shined. As I was sitting in the shoe shine chair, I could not believe my ears. The shoe shine man had a small radio sitting on a shelf and one of my songs, *"Sweet and Innocent"* began playing on the radio. It was an awesome feeling. I said to the man who was shining my shoes, "Hear that song? That's me!"

All he said in reply was, "Uh-huh."

After that unforgettable experience, James and I went on to see the Empire State Building and viewed the city from its top. I've been back to New York once since that time, but my first visit will always be the most memorable.

The emphasis placed on the theme of back to school was the main reason I was booked on the Dick Clark program, and it was to take advantage of the timing for record-buying kids. They would be going back to school the next week.

Although I had sung the song *"Back to School"* on national television, the radio stations all liked the other side of the record better and were playing *"Sweet and Innocent."* It was the same everywhere we went. When we got to Boston, *"Sweet and Innocent"* was one of the top forty tunes on the radio charts. As we made our way all over the New England states, my record was popular.

Within a week after the TV program, RCA Records contacted Judd and offered to buy my recording contract, along with the master tape of *"Sweet and Innocent."*

But Judd Records did not take their offer. Within another week, RCA released a new record by the former Sun Recording artist Roy Orbison, singing *"Sweet and Innocent."* That was the second chance I'd had to be with RCA Records. I was not too disappointed because Judd Records had given me everything anyone could have ever asked.

We continued on through the Midwest; over into Minnesota, Oklahoma, Texas, New Orleans, Mobile; and then home to Muscle Shoals. At every large city, I would meet the record distributors and did radio and television interviews.

Finally, it was good to be home after such a long and tiring trip. By now, Barbara was really getting a large tummy. According to my agreement with the record company, I could stay home with her until after the baby was born. Then I would be going on a tour, this time with Jerry Lee Lewis and other entertainers who were up-and-coming artists. The tour was called the Dick Clark Tour.

By this time, it was evident that my records, *"Back to School"* and *"Sweet and Innocent,"* were about to run their course and were not going to be big hits. About two years later, Rick Hall was beginning to have success with his FAME studio, and ask me to sing a new version of *"Sweet and Innocent"* as a demo recording. He managed to get Donnie Osmond to record the song; it sold over a million records.

In the meantime, Judd Record Company had already made plans for me to go to Houston, Texas, and record my next release. I was not asked for my opinion regarding this choice of recording location and did not understand the strategy of going to Houston rather than back to Nashville and allowing Buddy Killen to produce the second record as he had the last one.

I was disappointed about the decision and the fact that very little planning had been done in the selection of the songs to be recorded. This should have been a well-thought-out process, considering the success we'd had with the first record and the excellent exposure I'd received over the last few months around the country. However, I suppose the final decision was made by Judd Phillips, and he trusted the people in Texas who ran the studio and produced the session.

One positive thing about the studio was it had the latest equipment which allowed what is called overdubbing and recording on different tracks. In my mind, though, it was still not Nashville and did not have the professionalism and good players that we had before.

The session date was set, and plans were made to make the trip to Houston. Ironically, my mother's sister, Aunt Flora, lived in Houston and owned a dry-cleaning business. So, I thought it would be nice to take my mom and dad and little sister, Cala, to Texas with Barbara and me. They had never been far away from home, and it would be a good experience for them. By that time, I had a better car, a 1956 Buick, so we were off to Houston.

The songs that were decided for the new record were not as powerful as the others I had recorded in Nashville. But what did I know? I was just thrilled to be making records.

The song that was to be the A-side of the record was *"Lover's Plea,"* written by two people from Texas, Schular and Broussard, and published by Longhorn Music Incorporated. The other song, *"I'll Always be Yours,"* was a song that Tom Stafford and I had written. I had already formed a publishing company called Bobby Denton Music and was an affiliate of BMI (Broadcast Music Incorporated), the leading company for songwriters and music publishers at that time. So, I was the publishing company for that song.

After recording the new record, we made our way back to Alabama. My mom and dad and Cala had a good time with the visit and the experience of seeing a big city and all the sights in between.

When we got back home, I still had some time on my hands before the baby was to be born and I would be joining the *Dick Clark Tour*. Much of my time was spent working with Tom Stafford trying to put together a recording studio upstairs over his dad's drugstore. The studio would be for recording demo records of songs to pitch to record companies and other publishers. All I knew about studios was what I had observed seeing the inside of others and that they needed to be as soundproof as possible. That was a big job, and I began work trying to do it.

Later, we went to Nashville and purchased a tape recorder and a few items for the studio. It was not as good as the professional studio that was used for my latest records, but we thought it would do fine for demos. We went to Nashville in my '56 Buick and returned the same day, excited about the recording studio above the City Drug Store, which quickly became the number one hangout for all the boys around town who were aspiring to play music and write songs. We had fun experimenting with the equipment and being together.

My being married made me a little different from the others. They could play music and hang out as long as they wanted. But my responsibility as a husband and soon-to-be father compelled me to get home at reasonable times.

The time for Barbara's delivery was coming closer. I knew she was miserable and scared facing this first-time experience of giving birth. Finally, the time came, and we went to Colbert County Hospital, which is now Helen Keller Memorial Hospital, to have the baby. It seemed like forever waiting for the baby to come. Back then, the doctors did not have the technology to know the sex of the unborn child, and we were excited and wondered whether it would be a boy or a girl. We didn't really feel strongly about that aspect, as long as the mother and child were all right.

Our strong and healthy baby girl was born, and we were so happy. Becoming a parent brings on a feeling of serious responsibility almost immediately. We could tell that "we" was not just us, the couple, anymore but now also included the child, who was solely dependent upon us as parents.

The baby was born on December 21, 1958. She was sweet and beautiful. We had already talked about a name. So, within a short time after the birth, we named her Juliana Lee. The middle name was used to honor Barbara's mother, who had the same middle name.

Christmas was just a couple of days away, and we went home with our new gift from God, our little Julie. With the help of Barbara's mother and dad and the other members of our families, we made it fine. Friends and family had showered us with gifts for the baby, which helped us out a lot. We had an old used washing machine but did not have a clothes dryer, so the diapers had to be dried on a rack inside when the weather was too bad to hang them outside.

Little Julie was a prize and not a lot of trouble to care for. She began sleeping all night within a few days and was seldom sick. Our little family was content being at home. Although we didn't have a nice home and fancy car, we had love for each other.

All the while, in the back of my mind, I would remember the agreement with the record company and that I would have to leave soon to meet the others on the tour.

Within a few days, I received the call from the record company saying I would be picked up by a driver and carried to meet the group and tour with them. I didn't have a good feeling about leaving Barbara and Julie. I had grown up a lot over the last year, and my priorities had begun to change. But when the car came for me, I had to go. I had no choice.

Chapter Twelve

The tour was not as I had expected; it was not fun. I felt out of place and didn't hang out with the others much because they were all younger. After a couple of weeks, I felt a choice would have to be made again regarding my future. This was what I had always wanted to do, but it wasn't what I enjoyed doing. As I thought about my options, I knew that, whatever my final decision was, it would be life-changing.

I was homesick and miserable living on the road. It became clear that this was not the life for a person with a wife and young child at home. However, if I chose to quit the tour and go home, I would feel guilty for not fulfilling my commitment to the record company; and if I continued with the others, I would not be doing the right thing for my family.

After pondering my situation, my feeling did not change much. I called Barbara one day, and I could hear in her voice the desire for me to be home, but she never said she wanted me to come home. I just knew that's where I needed to be, for better or for worse. I told her about my dissatisfaction with the tour and that I would be coming home soon. Then I told the road manager that I wanted to quit the tour. So the next day, one of the employees of the company had to travel back to Florence for some reason, and I got a ride home with him.

My chance in music would be over now. The one thing I had always wanted to do would be gone forever and I didn't know how I would handle it. Somehow, the saying, *"Do the right thing, and you know what that is,"* kept sticking in my mind. I truly felt I was doing the right thing, although the future would be rough and rocky for me. Once again, I had to deal with the stigma of being unsuccessful in music, swallow my pride, and continue on with my life.

After I had left home to go on the tour, Rick Hall and Billy Sherrill joined up with Tom Stafford and began operating the studio above the City Drug Store that I had worked so hard helping to get together.

The next year was hard for us. I couldn't find a job anywhere around home. I went to Memphis looking for a job, but I was not successful.

A friend of mine called and said he knew of a job in sales located in Corinth, Mississippi, which was about forty-five miles west of Muscle Shoals. I applied for the job, and we moved into a small duplex apartment in Corinth. We were in a strange town with very little chance of success. However, living in an area where I was not well known was some benefit.

As the weeks passed, I did a lot of thinking about what was going to become of me and my life. I needed to do something to have the inner peace inside that I wanted so badly. Barbara's parents were Christians and very dedicated to God. Their faith had influenced her greatly as she grew up, and she would sometimes ask me about going to church. I had never spent time studying the Bible and had seldom attended church. However, as I became more mature, I could feel the need to do something regarding my spiritual condition. I needed the assurance that everything would turn out all right for me and my family. I knew that God could help me find the peace and assurance I needed. I needed God to come into my life and guide me through this uncertain time.

One morning, a man came by our house to ask if we had any laundry or dry-cleaning that he could pick up. He was a very nice man, and as we chatted for a few minutes, he asked me where we went to church. I told him that Barbara was a member of the Church of Christ, but we didn't attend church at all. I then went on to tell him that I might be interested in becoming a Christian someday. He then invited me to come by and talk with him and the minister of the Foot Street Church of Christ there in town to discuss my situation.

Later that day, I went by the church building, and we talked about what one must do to be saved. After talking with them for a long time, I accepted Christ as my Savior and was baptized for the forgiveness of my sins. After that experience, I felt a load had been lifted from me, and it seemed I was now prepared to deal with whatever problems I would be confronted with in life.

Within a few days my old friend and Barbara's uncle, Ralph Montgomery, contacted me again and asked if I would be interested in coming back home to work. He and a partner had a new business manufacturing aluminum windows and doors. He asked if I would travel around the region in North Alabama as a sales representative for the small company. Ralph said they would pay my expenses and mileage for my car, along with a salary of seventy-five dollars a week.

I quickly accepted the offer, and we moved back to the Muscle Shoals. We felt a lot better being closer to our families, especially Barbara's parents, who loved little Julie and helped us take care of her. There's no question that God was guiding me and opening doors for me.

Before going to Memphis and Corinth, I had already applied for a job at several places around home, including the job I had left before going to New York. I remembered the plant manager saying to me, "Bobby, if you ever need another job with us, let me know, and I will see what we can do." At that time, I'd thought, *"That will never happen."*

One night, after calling on all the building supply and hardware stores in the town of Pell City, Alabama, I called Barbara. She said the man from Stylon had called and asked if I would like to come back to work with them doing the same job I'd done before. I couldn't wait to take them up on their offer the next day. The only way to describe how I felt would be to compare myself with the story of the prodigal son in the Bible. He left home and had a wandering experience that didn't work out and was so happy to came back home.

When I'd left my job over a year before, I'd never thought I would be so excited to have it back again. I had experienced the dream of a lifetime and had seen and done things some people would have loved to do. However, I found out for myself what the full-time music business was really like and the price of experiencing it.

Although I was extremely thankful to have my old job back, I knew it would not provide the income I would like to have in order to provide for my family and have a better life. I had previously applied for a job at Ford Motor Company's local plant without success. I will always believe it was because I was interested in music. They thought I would not stick with the job, and they were probably right. However, now I was serious about a job with Ford, and every few days, I made contact with them about hiring me.

After several months, Ford called me, and I went to work for the company. Barbara and I thought this was as good as it could get—making over one hundred dollars a week and good benefits.

As time went by, I realized that, to have a better job in the plant, I would have to prepare myself to qualify for it. The best job in the plant, in my opinion, was that of quality control floor inspector. I noticed those guys walking around wearing clean clothes. They would check charts at the machines and look over the auto parts that were being made. I decided that job was the one I would like to have.

After asking questions regarding the position, I was told I could only get the job when an opening occurred, and the person who scored highest on the test was given the position. This was my new goal, to have the quality control floor inspector job. I began to stay late after work to study the instruments and gauges used. I would have to be able to properly read the parts blueprints and dimensional requirements to do the job. I stayed late at work studying these things one or two nights per week, preparing for the next opening.

Finally, a position came open. I knew I was ready for the challenge. I received a perfect score on the test; however, another fellow made a perfect score also. So he was given the job, as he had been with Ford longer than me. This was very disappointing.

Then another job came open within a few months, and this time, it was mine. I remained on that job for more than ten years before resigning in 1971 to devote myself full-time to the little business I had established, Bobby Denton Company.

With the good job at Ford and things going well, Barbara and I were happy raising our young family. On January 19, 1960, our second baby was born, thirteen months after Julie was delivered. This time we had a boy, and we named him Bobby Michael. Everyone always called him Mike.

That was not a good year for the automobile business, and Ford began to lay off workers, but I was among the lucky ones and was never laid off from work.

When little Mike was just about a year old, we noticed his eyes jumping and thought something was wrong. He was fitted with glasses at that young age and could see much better.

Later, he developed another problem—this time with his eyes sometimes crossing. We took him to Memphis to an ophthalmologist, and he later had surgery on his eyes. That was a frightening experience for us and required several trips to Memphis because of complications. Little Mike was tough and he did well coping with his eye problem as he grew up and began going to school.

With Julie and Mike only thirteen months apart, Barbara had her hands full, at first especially. She was dealing with two babies in diapers at the same time, carrying one and leading another. The two were almost like twins and loved each other immensely. The older Julie was always the little caregiving mother of the two.

After renting houses all around town, we purchased our first house on Highpoint Street, just east of Muscle Shoals. It was a new one-street subdivision of small brick homes. The house was nice; however, by today's standards, it was not great at all. We had three bedrooms, all hardwood floors, and one bathroom with ceramic tile. It had nice kitchen cabinets but no built-in appliances. The house had a single car carport, which was popular then, and electric heat—no central heat and air. We thought the house was very nice compared to the others we had lived in since being married. The total cost of the house was just over $6,000, and the payments were $67 per month, including property taxes and insurance.

It was conveniently located to the Ford plant but was not ideal for going into town, about five miles away. Within a year we had become tired of the inconvenience of driving into town and only having a small yard, which would be the same as living in town. So, we sold the house to a friend at Ford and bought another older house in a nice established neighborhood in Sheffield. Then in a couple of years, we purchased another new house in Muscle Shoals.

By that time, we realized that the location of schools would be a factor soon. Muscle Shoals was a fast-growing town and had new schools. Highland Park Elementary School was just a few blocks from our house, so Julie started school there one year, and Mike followed the next year.

My dad and mom had built a nice little house in Cherokee and were excited about having a better house for them and Cala. I remember Daddy talking about when he signed the papers for the twenty-year mortgage. He was sixty years old and the lender at the bank said, "Now Mr. Denton, I'm expecting you to personally bring us your last payment when you are eighty." They had a good laugh when he made the final payment twenty years later.

Barbara and I began to think about another child when Mike was now five years old. Things were going well with us. We thought another child would be good, and three children would be a nice family size for us. Julie and Mike were good little kids and got along so well together. When we told them we were going to see if God would send us a little baby, they were so excited.

In a few months, in 1965, our baby boy Roger came. He was beautiful and was born on my birthday, August 13. Little Roger was lovable and special in many ways. Julie and Mike were happy to have him as their baby brother.

Chapter Thirteen

When Roger was born, I was twenty-seven years old, and Barbara was twenty-five. With the three children, we decided to move to a house just outside of town again to give them more room to grow up. So, we bought a larger house with a one-acre lot.

I had always been interested in radio and TV towers and had a part-time business for several years installing them. One day in the early 60s, I was almost killed while installing a TV tower and antenna. It happened at a home on the side of a lake that had power lines running almost directly over the house. The man working with me was on the tower, and I was on the ground. As I pulled a wire to him, the wire came in contact with a high-voltage power line. I was sent tumbling several feet and was unconscious for a few minutes and could not get up. The 7,200 volts of electric power went through my body, and the current came out of the heel of one foot.

Back then, the communities did not have emergency rescue services. There was not even an ambulance as we know them today. A local funeral home was sent to take me to the hospital in a hearse they used to carry dead people. On top of that, they had no life-saving skills or equipment. I was treated at the hospital emergency room in Florence and later transferred to the hospital in Sheffield, where I remained for three days.

After the accident happened, I was told by people who had knowledge regarding electric shock that, if I were to experience this event again one hundred times, I would be killed ninety-nine of them. I was thankful to God for my survival and returned to work at Ford in two weeks.

With the large one-acre lot, keeping the grass mowed was a big job. We purchased a riding lawn mower after the first year, which made it easier. The front portion of the yard was steeply sloped, and caution was necessary while riding the mower for fear of it overturning. The lot's backyard was extremely level. It made a perfect place for the kids to play any type of sports.

On a few occasions while I cut the grass, Mike asked to drive the mower with me. I let him sit on my lap and steer the small mower around the yard a few times. Then later, when I was right there with him, he operated the mower by himself, going slow and carefully. Although he was only eleven at the time, he did a good job driving the mower for a brief period of time while I watched close by. Mike was never allowed to operate the mower without me being with him. Being a kid at heart, I knew driving the mower was fun for the boys, so I even let Roger steer the tractor while sitting on my lap sometimes.

My longtime friend Bobby Henry worked with me at Ford and was one of the best people who'd ever worked with me in the antenna business. One spring day we had gone to Savannah, Tennessee, to work on an antenna. We finished the job just after noon and were driving back. I had a two-way radio in my truck and a unit at home, so Barbara and I could communicate if needed. About halfway back from Savannah, the radio came on with someone trying to give me a message, but the signal was very weak, and it was not legible. I knew it wasn't Barbara, but it had to be coming from my house.

Then another transmission began, and it was a man's voice saying, "Bobby, if you can hear me, come home." This frightened me a lot. I tried to talk back to the person, who turned out to be my neighbor. I asked him what was wrong and he said, "Its Roger. He's hurt." At first, I was thinking he may have broken an arm or something, but when he said he was hurt badly by the lawn mower, I could hardly drive and was extremely worried.

Chapter Fourteen

After receiving the shocking news about the accident, we raced down the highway toward home. The radio transmission became clearer as we grew closer, and I was able to learn more about what had happened. I was told Roger would be taken to Huntsville and that he had been run over by the lawn mower. At this point, I became so upset Bob told me to pull over and let him drive, so I did. We were told Barbara was at Dr. John Mims's office in Tuscumbia and to come there.

The first thing I thought was we needed to get to Huntsville fast. So I asked them to call the airport and ask if Ralph Montgomery could fly us to Huntsville as soon as I got to Tuscumbia. By then, Ralph was co-owner of Muscle Shoals Aviation and had airplanes used for charter. I knew if Roger was being taken to Huntsville, he must be injured seriously.

Meanwhile, with Bob driving and speeding toward Tuscumbia, we arrived at the doctor's office within about thirty minutes.

When the accident happened, Barbara had reluctantly agreed for Mike to use the mower while she sat on the back patio watching him. In the meantime, the phone rang, and she went inside the house to answer. In a very short time, as she looked through the kitchen window, she heard the mower stop and Mike screaming. She ran to the yard and saw Roger's legs and feet, but his body was under the mower. Barbara was in total shock and lifted the mower up while she and Mike pulled him from beneath it. She thought he was dead.

The next-door neighbor, came over to find out what had happened. They noticed that Roger was alive and the neighbor drove the car while Barbara and Mike held Roger in the back seat. Our daughter, Julie, was visiting her grandparents at the time.

They stopped at Dr. John Mims's office, which was the first possible place to receive medical care. It was a blessing they stopped at the doctor's office because they carried him in the side door, and Dr. Mims was right there. Dr. John Mims was one of the most prominent doctors in the area, so I feel God directed the neighbor's actions.

The doctor immediately assessed Roger's injuries and called the local funeral home to provide an ambulance to transport him to Huntsville Hospital, which was about seventy miles away. The doctor knew Roger needed a neurosurgeon in order to have any possibility of survival. The blade had sliced through his brain down from the top of his head, through his face and mouth. A large portion of the skull bone was torn away, and he had a large cut down his midsection.

When I arrived at the doctor's office, I saw Barbara covered with blood and crying, "Don't let my baby die."

Dr. Mims had already left with Roger in the ambulance for Huntsville. He left his office full of patients and rode with Roger all the way, administering an IV and doing all he could to control the bleeding.

The highway to Huntsville was two-lane at that time, and the Tuscumbia police gave them an escort out of town, and called ahead for the towns on the route to expect them soon. Dr. Mims's office called Huntsville Hospital and alerted them regarding the incoming emergency. The hospital contacted the appropriate doctors, and they were standing by waiting for his arrival.

Shortly after I arrived at the doctor's office, Barbara and I were carried to the Muscle Shoals Airport by my brother Johnny and my sister Vera, who had heard about the accident and came to the doctor's office. All the way from Tuscumbia to the hospital, Barbara and I cried and prayed that our little boy would be all right. When we arrived at the Huntsville Airport, a police car was waiting on the runway, and carried us to the hospital. The coordination of this event was unbelievable.

Roger, being the baby, was special, not because I loved him more than the other two children, but he was born on my birthday. When we reached Huntsville Hospital Emergency Room, Dr. Mims was there in the waiting room. He was so nice and talked with us about Roger. We could tell Dr. Mims was very concerned but didn't want to show it because we were already upset ourselves.

By that time, the word about the accident had spread all around the Shoals area, and some of our close friends came to the hospital to support us. It seemed like we waited for hours to get an update about Roger. Dr. Mims returned home with the ambulance and wished us well. We were very thankful for his kindness and dedication to come with Roger and care for him. Without his help, Roger would have not made it through this ordeal.

We were not allowed to see Roger at all until the next day, but the doctors came out to talk to us after the long surgery. We hung on to every word they said as we struggled to control our emotions. They told us he might not live through the night, and it was a slim chance for him to recover.

At that point, I thought our lives were over. I could not believe this was happening to us. In my mind I said, *Now God can fix this, and He's just going to have to do it.* Then, while a few of our friends sat with Barbara, my friends Wayne Green and Ralph Montgomery took me walking on the sidewalk outside the hospital. The words of the doctor kept sounding in my ears, and I could not accept their projections for our little boy's well-being. Wayne and Ralph did their best to console me, but my emotions were almost uncontrollable.

We all sat through the night, waiting for word from Roger. They told us that, if he made it through the night, we could see him in the morning. All through the night we prayed to God and asked Him to help us. I made up my mind that God was going to hear from me, and I knew He had the power to save my boy's life.

The next morning, at 8:00 a.m., I called the local newspaper in Florence and told them I wanted to run an ad in the paper. The lady asked me what I wanted the ad to say, and I said, "Just say, 'Pray for Roger Denton.'" The small ad ran the next day, and the churches and people all over the Shoals area began praying for Roger. The newspaper ran a news story about the accident also.

Later that morning, as we sat in the waiting room of the intensive care unit, one of the doctors came out and said we could go in to see Roger for just a minute. He said, "I don't know if he can hear you or will know who you are, but please try not to show your emotions. If he can hear you crying or being emotional, that may upset him more."

His head was completely bandaged; only one eye was not covered with the bandage, and it was swollen shut. Barbara and I slowly entered the quiet room and held each other as we stood by his bed and looked at him. Then I took his little hand into mine and said, "Roger, this is Daddy. If you can hear me, squeeze my hand."

He began squeezing my finger over and over again. We were so happy and I felt that God was going to help us. We stayed a few minutes, talking to him and encouraging him, saying he would be OK and that we loved him.

Barbara and I were allowed to see him again that night, and we went to the hospital chapel to pray several times that day and through the days that followed.

As the days went by, we began to have more hope, and we were visited by numerous friends from home. The Tuscumbia Church of Christ, where we were members, offered up constant prayers for Roger, as did all the other churches in the area back home. Roger made steady progress and surprised the doctors with his recovery. When the day came for him to be transferred from the ICU into a room, we felt confident regarding his recovery. We both stayed in his room around the clock, sleeping briefly, using the hospital chair and a small cot.

I was lucky having my job at Ford because the company allowed me to take leave time while I was away in Huntsville. We worried about Julie and Mike not being with us, but we knew they would be fine staying with Barbara's parents.

Within two weeks, we brought Roger home. We were so humbled and thankful for our prayers being answered. Roger had a turban-looking bandage covering his head. It had to be changed each day after we left the hospital. But Barbara had watched the nurses do it many times, so she performed that duty every day for the next few years as Roger went through several related operations to replace the missing skull and complications that followed.

After the neurosurgeon was satisfied with the brain repair, most of the remaining work was done by a plastic surgeon, who did a remarkable job.

Without going into lengthy and graphic details, Roger was a miracle who God saved for a special purpose. He went to school his first year using a special speaker phone hookup with his classroom. Roger could hear the class proceedings and could answer questions from the teacher by pressing a button on the speaker box. We thought this was high technology back then. This worked well, and he felt a part of being in school. Because of further surgery, he attended school wearing his head bandage the next year without any trouble. He was not intimidated by his looks, and the other children loved him and were never hostile toward him.

A few months later, Barbara asked me to look at Roger's forehead and see if I thought it was all right. His forehead was discolored and puffy where the doctors had replaced his missing skull with a man-made substance. His head had looked very good after the procedure, but something was now wrong.

We called the doctor in Huntsville, and he recommended bringing Roger to see him as soon as possible. We carried our boy back to Huntsville, and the doctor said his body had rejected the material' it would have to be removed. This was devastating to us. We didn't want to go through this situation again, but we had no choice.

The surgery required would remove the plastic-like material from a large portion of his forehead. Later, it would be replaced with two of his ribs grafted into place. With several subsequent operations over the next few years,

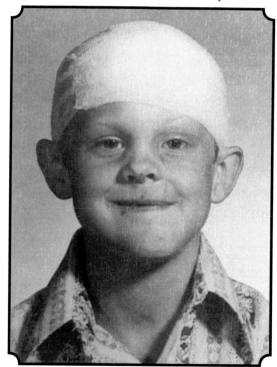

Little Roger

it was very trying on us, especially Roger, but he continued to be brave. During the coming years, we did our best to raise the children while struggling financially.

My God and I

Chapter Fifteen

While I was away on a business trip to Burlington, Iowa, Barbara's dad passed away suddenly. I immediately flew home to be with Barbara and the family. Eugene was the finest man I had ever known, and he was so good to me and my family. He never had a lot of material possessions, but he had a life record of kindness and love for everyone. Eugene P. Jeffreys will always be remembered as a good man who loved others.

After the death of Barbara's dad, her mother had no income at all. Most people have never realized the problems a widow has without experiencing it firsthand. Eugene was fifty-two years old, and Myrtie Lee was fifty. He only had enough insurance to cover the funeral and related expenses. She did not qualify for social security or other benefits at her age. She was not allowed to draw from his social security before she turned sixty-two, which meant she would have no income or health benefits for the next twelve years. She managed to get a job paying minimum wage but had no insurance. Medicare was only available for people sixty-five and older.

By then, I needed someone to answer the phone and look after the office. Although Myrtie Lee had no experience in this area of work and had limited office skills, she went to work for Bobby Denton Company, which was able to pay her a living salary and provide the company Blue Cross insurance coverage. She was a very conscientious employee and everyone loved having her with us. The young men who worked for me called her Mamaw, as did the grandchildren. That became her name to all of us in the future.

The next few years were fairly normal for the family. Our teenage daughter Julie was a cheerleader at the high school, and we attended all athletic actives to support her. I didn't realize then how beautiful it was to come home and see the cheerleaders practicing in the backyard and the boys, Mike and Roger, shooting basketball in the paved parking area in the back.

When Mike was fifteen-years old, we bought him a new bicycle. Our street was a dead end and about a quarter of a mile long. It was a good street for the kids to ride, but they had strict instructions not to go beyond our street on to the main road.

After a few weeks, one day Mike asked if he could ride his bicycle to the store located about a mile away on the main road. I had refused to allow him to go several times before, but after thinking about it and knowing the store was only a short distance down the road, I said yes, with instructions to watch out for the traffic and be careful. Mike was a strong, experienced rider, and I thought it was fine for him to go on the short trip to the store. It would be fun for him.

After he had been gone for several minutes, a woman came to the house and said, "Come quickly. Mike has been hit by a car."

We rushed to the location, and as we came near the site, we saw lots of cars parked on the side of the road. A friend of mine came and met our car and said Barbara, Julie, and Roger should stay in the car while I went to see about Mike. They wanted to go see about him also, but it would not have been good for them to see him at that time.

I had no idea what to expect as I ran up the road. I saw a car off the road, sitting in the edge of a field. And when I got close, I saw Mike and his bicycle crumpled and lying behind the car. He was conscious, and as I approached him, I said to him, "Son, I am so sorry."

Mike was being very brave; I could see that his legs were broken, and he was in terrible pain. Because he and the bicycle were at the back of the car, it was clear that the car had hit him on the road and rolled him beneath it, through a fence and into the field.

By that time, an am- bulance arrived with the police. This time, it was a real ambulance, not

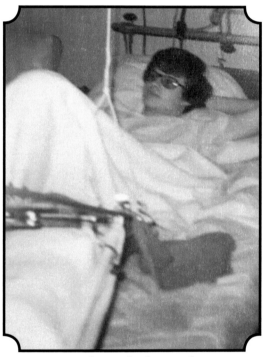

Mike in the hospital

the funeral home hearse I had experienced before. Colbert County Hospital had purchased the vehicle just a short time before to serve their emergency room. I asked a friend to go to my car and tell Barbara that Mike was going to the hospital, and I was riding with him.

Mike was taken into the emergency room and treated. He

was later sent to ICU where he stayed several days. He was critically injured, with fifteen broken bones and internal injuries.

The lady driving the car was a teacher at Colbert Heights School. She was traveling in the same direction as Mike when the car hit him. We felt sorry for her because we knew she would not have done this on purpose. Mike had several surgeries over the next several days and was placed in traction while he recovered. He endured this situation well, and we gave him all our support; he spent ninety-nine days in the hospital before coming home. He was determined not to let his injuries keep him down.

With these horrific events occurring in our lives, I wondered if I was being punished for some reason. I didn't understand why we were having so much trouble when others may not experience near as much in their entire lifetime. But I thought how lucky we had been to come through these tragedies and still have our children. I believe everyone reacts differently in dealing with despair, as well as prosperity. Some cannot handle power or financial success or adversity. Some people turn away from God, and some turn toward Him.

Our faith is all we have when we are convinced that a situation is beyond our control. Only our faith can give us the peace of mind needed to cope with serious problems. We do not have to look far to find people who have problems worse than ours. I truly believe that a person who has faith in God can endure troubles and adversity much better than those who do not know Him.

However, if our faith is strong, we may still have extreme problems in our lives. I have had people tell me many times that God would not allow us to suffer beyond that which we can bear.

That's not what the Bible says. What about the Christians who were put to death because of their faith? Consider the story of Job in the Bible. He lost everything he had but refused to blame God. The scripture these people are referring to is, I Corinthians: 10:13, and it is clearly talking about temptation. The scripture says that we will not be tempted beyond a way of escape. When the rain comes, it rains on the bad man's farm just as it does on the good man's farm.

Julie began driving after she was sixteen, and we bought her a new Chevrolet that she loved very much. She drove it for years until it was worn completely out. Then Mike was next to get a car. He wanted a sportier model, so we got him a new Pontiac Firebird.

While the kids were learning to drive, I tried to teach them some of the things they might experience while driving. One of the most important things was that of running off the pavement. If they ever felt that happen and quickly oversteered the car back on to the road, they could have a bad accident. That is one of the most common causes of teenage accidents.

Raising two teenagers at the same time was a great learning experience. One day, after discussing some does and don'ts with them, they said to me, "Daddy, you just don't understand."

"You're right, I don't," I said. "I have never been a daddy of teenagers before. And you have never been a teenage before. So we will have to learn how to do this together."

When Mike had only had his new car for a few weeks, we were all going to church for Wednesday night Bible study, and Mike left early to pick up his friend to go to church with him. Within a few minutes, as the rest of us were about to leave the house, the phone range. It was Mike.

He said, "Daddy, you're not going to believe this, but I have just hit a kid down here on Frankfort Road."

He was right. I could hardly believe it.

We rushed to the scene and found Mike's car sitting on the street and a big healthy boy about twelve years old lying in a yard on the other side of the street. We quickly went over to check on him, and his mother was giving him a strong talking to about crossing the street and not being careful. He was in pain, but his only injury was a broken leg. That was bad, but we were thankful it wasn't worse. The police said it was unavoidable, and there was no speeding involved. We visited him every day at the hospital, and our insurance company paid his hospital and doctor bills, along with a few thousand dollars of repairs to Mike's car. Although Mike had problems with his legs and knees as a result of his accident on his bicycle, he insisted on playing football. He was number 74, a big healthy kid, and did a good job playing right tackle for the Colbert Heights Wildcats. As we watched the games, we always sat in fear that he'd be injured; and he was a few times but never seriously.

Julie had been in love with number 6, Philip McCreary, on the Colbert Heights football team for years. She graduated from high school and didn't want to go to college. She went to work at a local bank and was very happy. Until she was married, she always stayed close and came home from dates with Philip by curfew time. Julie and Philip were a committed young couple and never dated anyone else.

Roger continued to do well and was growing up as smart as a whip and making good grades in school. His favorite pastime was riding his go-cart on his little racetrack out back at the edge of the field behind our house.

Chapter Sixteen

As I became older and more mature, my thoughts became attracted to community service and government. I can't explain why one wants to serve as an elected official, but I just felt drawn to give it a try. At first, I thought about the county school board, but decided that I would be more suited to serving as a member of the Colbert County Commission. It was a part-time job and only paid $250 per month. I looked into the possibility and was sure that my name recognition was good because of my music and business background. I made having a full-time doctor in the emergency room at the Colbert County Hospital my number one issue and promised to get that done if elected.

My opponent was an old friend and a good person who was running for another term. I didn't know about any of the old-school politics, so I just got out there and was myself, asking people to vote for me. As it turned out, he and I were the only candidates running in that district, so that meant there would be no runoff after the primary, and no opposition in the general election later that November.

I was thirty-eight years old, and he was about ten years older. He certainly had more experience and knowledge about government. Now, after serving two years as county commissioner, and thirty-two years as state senator, I have determined that getting elected is all about if people like you and trust you.

After being elected to the Colbert County Commission in spring 1976, I was humbled by the public's trust in me and began reading the paper and listening to local news more to be aware of things going on in the county. It seemed like forever from the time I was elected in the spring until the time I would take office in mid-January.

Serving on the Colbert County Commission was exciting. The challenges were many, and I wanted to bring a more progressive element to the governing body of the county. The county was completely debt free, which was very unusual for counties in Alabama.

My two years as a member of the Colbert County Commission were very good for me. Times and technology were changing, and a lot of things needed to be done to keep up with the public needs.

Colbert County was one of the first counties in the state to purchase a computer system. With the leadership of then tax collector, Hank Rand, who developed software to have the ad valorem taxes computerized, the computer was a tremendous benefit. Dozens of counties throughout Alabama purchased the program from Colbert County to implement in their tax collection system.

Several other things were accomplished during that time in addition to the new computer system. We built a new modern health department building and constructed a large county water system serving most portions of the rural area.

I continued to operate my antenna business and became the largest antenna dealer in the southeast. We expanded into more commercial work for Motorola and General Electric two-way radio system towers, AM and FM radio station towers, and athletic playing field lighting. With all I had going on, one would think I would not be thinking about further involvement in politics.

I love people and the pleasure of serving them in a public service capacity. So, I became interested in politics at the state level and soon began to think that I would like to serve as state senator for Northwest Alabama, which was also considered as a part-time job. When I mentioned the possibility of running to others, some would say it was a very big district and would require a lot of money and hard work. However, in my mind, I knew I was very well known throughout the district and would do well.

A Senate district in Alabama is made up of three House of Representative districts and consists of about 150,000 people. Senate District 1 in which I would run in was made up of two House seats in Lauderdale County and one consisting of parts of Colbert and Franklin Counties at that time. The old-time politicians thought, since most of the voters were in Lauderdale County, a candidate who lived in Colbert County couldn't win.

Somehow, I felt that I was being drawn to run and that this was something God had planned for me to do. Along with the incumbent in the race, there was a twelve-year veteran of the House of Representatives who had good name recognition. He was an astute attorney who had experience in the legislative process. The feeling of the so-called political experts was that the incumbent needed to be replaced, but they thought the candidate from Lauderdale County would win.

I was not knowledgeable in high-rolling politics and didn't know much about the legislative process. I didn't know about special interest groups who were interested in working for or against a candidate. I just believed the voters would choose me.

My only funding came from individuals and small businesses around the area and one large group who had never taken an active part in supporting a candidate for the State Senate before. They were the Alabama Farm Bureau, who later became ALFA. They gave me about $8,000 and provided technical help and assistance, along with a person to help me in the campaign.

When the primary election was over, I received the most votes of the three candidates and had spent the least amount of money. A runoff would be held between the incumbent and me in three weeks, and that was the hardest part, but I won the final race.

George Wallace was the governor, and Fob James had just been elected to take his place in January. But I (as per the Alabama Constitution), a newly elected state senator, took the office immediately after being elected.

The next year, I made one of the biggest mistakes I had ever made. I expanded my business by buying a building and property at a new location. The timing could not have been worse. It was the beginning of the 80s, and Ronald Reagan had just taken office. The economic recession came, and interest rates went as high as 22 percent, as I struggled to make the situation work out. With me being gone three days a week lots of the time, the business suffered, and I knew another life-changing decision would have to be made. I was going broke fast, and I knew it was going to be over soon. Another big dream I had nurtured for most of my life was going to come to an end.

The choices I had were to go bankrupt or liquidate all the inventory, equipment, and property and then try to pay off the balance when I could find another job. Although I later thought it may have been better to have used the bankruptcy law and gotten away clean and free of residual debt, that was just not the way I was raised. I wanted to make sure all my remaining debts were paid in full. So, when the decision was made to liquidate and close the business, I felt somewhat relieved and set out to make the best of it. One of the first things I did was to spread the word around that I was looking for a job and was going out of business.

Later, Ed Mauldin, a longtime friend and founder of First Colbert Bank, contacted me regarding a job at the bank. One of the first things I told him was that all my experience with banks had been on the borrowing side of the desk. He said, "That's OK. We wouldn't need you to make loans; we need you to get new business for the bank." I had no idea what a business development officer was.

After a few meetings with Mr. Mauldin at the bank, I accepted the job and was very thankful for the opportunity. I worked hard to dispose of all the business assets and had a large negative balance. Mr. Mauldin and the bank worked with me to structure a loan to cover it all. The loan was paid back in full over the next several years through monthly payments. I continue to have very fond memories of the people who had faith in me and helped me through this ordeal in my life.

I was employed as vice president at the bank, which later became Bank Independent for five years. The bank experienced exceptional growth during the years I was with them and continues to be one of the leading community banks in Alabama.

My God and I

Chapter Seventeen

The 80s were filled with happy and sad times. My dear mother died after an extended illness, on February 20, 1982, leaving my dad living alone in their little house in Cherokee. Our daughter, Julie, was married to Philip in a nice wedding at the Church of Christ in Tuscumbia. I was very proud of them after so many years of being devoted to each other. Julie had often said that all she ever wanted was to be a wife and a mother. Although she has proven to be an excellent wife, she was never able to have children. But I am convinced that God had other plans and has allowed her to be the loving and caring angel she has always been to others.

Later, our son Mike was married and gave us our first grandson, Matthew, and then a granddaughter, Ashley.

Then our youngest son, Roger, was married to Devona Pounders and they had our third grandchild, Jordan who is now a professional guitar player.

Like all grandparents, we were filled with joy seeing the grandchildren grow and be a part of our lives. We are very proud of them all, as they are proving themselves and developing their adulthood further and raising their families.

My work in the State Senate was very involved; I served on numerous committees. Because of the recession in the early

80s, the economic condition in the Shoals area was devastated. Several things needed done in order to transition the area and make it more diverse in terms of employment. Over the years, several large industries provided thousands of well-paying jobs, and the area had not looked beyond that time of prosperity to prepare for the future.

Bobby presiding over the Senate

I have chosen not to divulge in this writing the extent of my involvement in the changes that have occurred over the more than thirty years that I served as County Commissioner and State Senator for the area. I have always thought political leaders should not brag on themselves and take credit for what the people elected them to do; rather, after they're gone, should they be due credit for things they have accomplished, that would be more proper.

When I entered the political arena, I could never in my wildest dreams have thought that I, as a poor sharecropper's son, would be elected to be a member of the State Senate, and to be the longest continuous serving member of that august institution. All those years I spent believing that everyone was smarter than me because I didn't make good grades in school and never went to college until I was a grandfather kept me humble while going about my duties in government.

After all these years dealing with the highest levels of elected officials, I have decided that many of them are not as smart as they think they are and may even be a legend in their own mind. I always thought the people making the decisions in Washington and in our State and local governments, knew what they were doing. The sad thing is, sometimes they don't. However, for the most part, most people serving us in government are good and smart, well-meaning individuals who want to do the right things.

When I had been employed with the bank just over five years, the local junior college advertised for a new position—director of development. The college, Northwest Alabama State Junior College, had its main campus located in Phil Campbell, about thirty miles south of Muscle Shoals and a satellite campus at Tuscumbia, which only had about two hundred students. The job would be overseeing the development of a foundation for the college, as well as rebuilding the Tuscumbia campus to attract more students. I applied for the position, which offered a better salary and benefits than I currently had at the bank.

I was interviewed by a committee at the college and was recommended to the president, Dr. Charlie Britnell, for the job. The position was very challenging, and I took it on with high hopes of success for the small college. I worked with a consultant from Santa Fe Community College in Gainesville, Florida, and studied foundation development to begin the process of establishing a foundation for our college, which was a 501(c)(3) nonprofit corporation. Within a year, we had a full slate of board members for the foundation. They were the top people in the college service area.

The process of making the community aware of the college and what it had to offer was my first purpose. Then the ultimate goal was to raise large amounts of money to provide scholarships for the students and financial support for the college. This concept had never been done as an organized and professional effort and became very successful.

Over the years, the two-year colleges began going through a transition of mergers and reorganization. The colleges were becoming more attractive to the modern-day students, who in years past had not given the junior colleges much thought. Up until these years, the system did not have good credibility with the public. Published stories about kids taking classes at a junior college and then finding out that the credits would not transfer to a four-year college did considerable damage. The state school board finally decided action needed to be taken to correct this problem. First of all, the two-year schools had been a stepchild of our education system since they were started. Under the early George Wallace administrations, they were very political, being overseen by the elected state school board.

With the leadership of the chancellor of the two-year system, all junior colleges began to offer only transferable courses, and all the colleges were given a time frame to become an accredited community college. This action, approved by the state school board, began to change the image of these schools drastically.

As I approached the final year of my eighth term in the Senate, I thought back on the long days and the trying round trips of over four hundred miles, and wondered why I did it. This is one of the hardest questions for a person who serves in politics to answer. I'm sure there are several fancy replies that could be given regarding this question. It could be because of power or ego or other things; it isn't money, for sure.

I have a neighbor who asked me if I planned to seek another term of office. After telling him that I was not sure yet, he said, "Well, you'll have a real good retirement." That's what almost everyone in Alabama thinks. But the truth is, (*as per the 1901 Alabama State Constitution*) a member of the Alabama State Legislature has no retirement or any other benefits for his or her service. Most people think they do, but, they don't, no matter how long they may serve. I'm not complaining at all; it has been a major chapter in my life that I am very thankful for. To come from where I was born and to do all the things that I have done is a blessing for me, and I humbly appreciate the trust the people have given me by allowing me to serve them.

I thought after thirty-two years in the Alabama State Senate, and two years as a member of the Colbert County Commission, it was time for someone new to take the position. There were many good people who could do it well.

My God and I

Chapter Eighteen

My dad passed away in his sleep on February 13, 1991. He had struggled for more than two years from small strokes, which gradually affected his ability to talk. His walking and regular activities continued to be normal, but over time, he finally became unable to speak at all. He was ninety-two years old when he passed and was a kind and happy man for his entire life. His love for music was one of his greatest pastimes.

After my mother's death, Daddy lived alone in Cherokee for several years. Later as he grew older, the children all kept him at our homes at times. He soon became tired of living with others and said he would like to live at the nursing home where my mother had lived a few years before her death. He enjoyed being with other people.

Daddy's funeral was somewhat unusual. At his request, one of his old friends, who played the banjo like he did, played the banjo. It was a touching experience. Everyone knew the old-time song that was played gave a perfect example of who my father was. Along with the banjo tune, the funeral home played two songs that I had recorded a few years earlier, "Peace in the Valley" and "Just a Closer Walk with Thee." I had recorded the two gospel songs at Wishbone Studios in Muscle Shoals as a promotional project for the Alabama Music Hall of Fame.

The history of music in the Muscle Shoals area has deep roots, and the area has become famous all over the world for its beginning by some kids who loved to play music. They had no idea that history was being made through their efforts, but the humble beginnings of a lot of people established the area as a great music icon in the world. Numerous stories about the several recording studios and the dozens of people who have made the music of Muscle Shoals what it was and still is today could be written.

Soon after I was elected to the state senate in 1978, a few of my old friends in the music business around the area met with me to talk about the possibility of establishing an Alabama Music Hall of Fame and locating it in the Muscle Shoals area. We decided to try and pass legislation for its creation. Our local legislative delegation, state representatives Tom Coburn, Joe Goodwin, and Nelson Starkey, were all very involved with the effort. We all directed the bill through the legislature, and it became law. So, then we had a hall of fame; but it was only a board to be appointed by the Governor. The legislature did not provide funding for the operations or a building. All that came after years of hard work and political struggles.

Through the ensuing years, finally a state bond issue provided the funds to build a nice building located on Highway 72 in Tuscumbia. The Alabama Music Hall of Fame is now a fine museum highlighting all the people in our state who made a contribution to our musical heritage. The Music Hall of Fame has functioned well over the years with very limited funding other than admission ticket sales and small fund raisers. The state has provided a small amount of funds over the years, but the funds for the arts and museums have never been a high priority for most governors and legislators.

A few years after the building was completed, some of the board members asked the governor to appoint me as a member of the board of directors. It was a high honor for me to serve. The terms were for six years, but members could have the possibility of being reappointed for future terms. The next governor replaced me after my first term was up. I have always thought the board should not be political, but it has always been that way.

One day, while talking with my good friends the late Jimmy Johnson and Ava Aldridge about music, the subject of my recording an album and allowing the proceeds to go to the hall of fame came up. It was 1996, and I had not sung in years, but I said I would love to try and make a gospel album. I agreed to raise the money to pay for the expense if they would produce it as their contribution. They both quickly said yes, and the project was launched.

Within a few weeks, we had a first-class gospel album. Jimmy and Ava arranged to get the best musicians in the area to do the session. We cut the basic soundtracks at Rick Hall's FAME Studio in Muscle Shoals and did the vocals at Rain Tree Studio in Sheffield, owned by Lenny LeBlanc. And we did most overdub recording at Muscle Shoals Sound Studio in Sheffield, which was operated by Roger Hawkins. The title of the CD is *My God and I*, it was distributed by Books-A-Million and The Walmarts throughout the south. The CD sold well and raised money for the hall of fame.

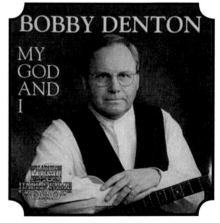

After the CD was released, I became more confident singing again after forty years. I purchased a small sound system and began performing for small audiences around the area, singing with the soundtracks mostly to senior citizens. They loved the old-time gospel songs especially.

In the meantime, Jimmy and Ava helped me to record a track of my first record that I made in the 50s, "*A Fallen Star*," so I sang it on the programs also. After that experience, I continued to record songs and eventually recorded a total of eighty-eight songs during my lifetime.

Chapter Nineteen

Our son Mike, who was badly injured in the car/bicycle accident when he was fifteen years old, later began to have problems with his knee. He was now forty-two years old. His orthopedic doctor suggested he would need a knee replacement, and Mike took it under consideration. He talked with us about making the decision, and I suggested he go to Birmingham to the Sports Medicine Clinic for the surgery. He didn't like the idea of going to Birmingham and liked his doctor here at home. Mike trusted him and felt comfortable with him doing the replacement.

The procedure was done, and he went through a long recovery, with therapy, for several weeks. It seemed the knee was not healing as it should; but like most men, Mike didn't return to the doctor to complain.

In the meantime, Mike and his wife divorced after several years of drifting apart. This was very upsetting for all the family, and Mike took it hard, adjusting to a different life, living alone in an apartment in Tuscumbia.

As the weeks went by, his knee wasn't doing well. It was red and swollen, and we could tell something was wrong, but Mike continued to resist pursuing the problem. As he tried hard to maintain a normal lifestyle, the knee was always in his way. The company he worked for would not let him return to work unless he could do the job without restrictions. Luckily, he was able to maintain his medical insurance and received a small medical leave income from his employer.

Mike loved his mother and grandmother especially, and they talked several times every day. His grandmother, who was Barbara's mother, Myrtie Jeffries, or Mamaw as we all called her, lived about a block away from Mike's apartment, and he would visit with her often.

One day, Mike called Barbara and said, "Mama, I have something really wrong with my knee. I can't get out of bed."

Barbara rushed over to see about him and immediately knew he had to see the doctor. His knee was blood red and swollen very large. They went to see the doctor, and he drew a large vial of liquid from the knee and said, "Take him to the hospital immediately."

The next day he told Mike his knee had a bad infection and the prosthetic would have to be removed. After Mike had checked into the Helen Keller Memorial Hospital, it was very clear he had a very serious problem with his knee.

The joint was removed, and they began giving him massive amounts of antibiotics, trying to kill the infection. He lay helpless for days without a knee joint and with it heavily bandaged. The doctor consulted with the infectious disease specialist in Birmingham, and said he was doing all that could be done.

Another two weeks passed as we stood by him thinking somehow, he would show improvement. But he didn't improve. We were very worried, and the doctor finally arranged for him to be transferred to UAB Hospital in Birmingham.

The hospital in Birmingham contemplated how he should be transported and decided to send their ambulance with a nurse and doctor for him.

After about two hours, the crew arrived and went in to see Mike to premedicate him for the trip. After they finished, and were about to leave for Birmingham, we went in to see Mike and assure him that we were coming right behind the ambulance with him to Birmingham.

Mike said to me, "Daddy, I don't feel good about going to Birmingham."

We only had a few brief moments, and I asked him if he was OK with Jesus.

He said, "Yes."

The trip to Birmingham was fast and scary, not knowing what the future held for our son.

As we went through the two weeks at the hospital at home, we heard the word infection dozens of times, but the words staph infection was never used by the doctors or nursing personnel. That's what our son had, though, and they knew it, but they didn't want to talk about it. Staph infection is an infection caused by bacteria of the genus *staphylococcus*, and there are more than thirty species. According to the Centers for Disease Control and Prevention Health Care Association, these infections account for an estimated 1.7 million infections and an about 99,000 associated deaths each year in American hospitals.

Upon our arrival at UAB Hospital, Mike was rushed to the intensive care unit. There were several doctors who cared for him; however, in a large teaching hospital, one never knows who is in charge.

The doctors knew Mike was in trouble and quickly began treatment with high-powered medicine. After several days without improvement, they tried the newest, more powerful, experimental medicines with no success.

Barbara and I stayed with Mike around the clock, seven days a week, waiting and sleeping in the waiting room. Later, after a few weeks, we were able to get a room inside the hospital for out-of-town people to use. We took turns using the room for sleeping and taking showers.

I know it may seem that we were hovering over him and may have been overreacting to the situation given our son was a forty-two-year-old adult. But who would be with him and care for him other than his family? Barbara and I, along with his beloved sister, Julie; his brother, Roger; and Barbara's sister, Carolyn, gladly took on that responsibility. It didn't matter what age he was; he was our son who we loved, and we would have gladly taken his place in the hospital bed. But that was impossible, so all we could do was pray for him, be with him, talk to him, and let him know we were there and loved him.

Week after week passed without any improvement in his condition. He developed sepsis, which is a condition in which the body is fighting a severe infection that has spread through the bloodstream. The doctors placed him in an induced coma, which is done often with seriously ill patients, using a ventilator or breathing tube. They say that this helps the patients to heal better. It may do that, but I am convinced that this technique is used more for the medical personnel than for the patient. The patients cannot talk, move, or anything, but

I believe they can hear. Can you imagine lying there in that paralyzed condition, hearing the doctors and nurses and family members talking about you? Who knows what they hear? They may hear the doctors saying, "He's not going to live." I believe the induced coma is overused in hospitals and should only be done as a very last resort.

I thought about our son Roger years ago as he squeezed my finger to respond to my talking to him. That meant everything to us. If Mike could have responded to us in any way it would have made the situation much easier. I shudder to think of the pain he must have gone through.

Later his organs began shutting down; his kidneys and liver finally stopped functioning, and he was placed on a dialysis machine. After seven weeks at UAB, with strong advice from the doctors, Barbara and I reluctantly agreed to stop the life support.

In the final seconds of his life, Barbara and I were leaning over on him and holding him close to us when he took two deep breaths and was gone. His eyes remained open, so I closed them with my fingers. To say the least, we were devastated. It was 4:30 p.m. on Friday, July 2, 2002.

I said to Barbara, "I sure wish we could see the angels."

The Bible says that angels will come and take us when we die, and I'm sure they came, but we could not see them.

My friend Wayne Green drove Barbara and me home later that night as the other family members followed us.

I have been to church and read the Bible a lot, but I continue to not fully understand the mysteries of death and the afterlife. We all have heard great preachers give sermons and read commentaries of the Bible by learned people, but it's still not completely clear to me.

However, after thinking about it, I can realize why God didn't reveal everything there is to know about these matters. We are human beings, and the wisdom of God is so powerful and far beyond our thinking we can't understand it. I believe what we are told in the Bible is all He wanted us to know. Why would He give us every detail about death and heaven before we die to experience it? He tells us that He has prepared for us a place that we are unable to imagine. God deals with us through faith, and we must have faith in Him to provide all these things that we can't know or understand in this life.

Mike's funeral was held at the Tuscumbia Church of Christ on July 5, 2002. The church was filled with family and friends from home and from Montgomery. Several of my Senate colleagues and staff people were there, along with Governor Don Siegelman and other elected officials. He was buried at the Tuscumbia Oakwood Cemetery in a plot next to where his Grandmother Jeffreys would be buried a few years later.

No one can ever understand what it's like to lose a child without experiencing it. The sadness and despair gradually get better, but the loss can never completely leave our mind. We did our best to cope with Mike's death and not go around feeling sorry for ourselves. I find now after several years it is comforting to talk about him and the good memories. If you have lost a child and someone says to you, "I understand," ask them when they lost their child, because if they have not lost a child, they have no idea what it's like, and they don't understand. I sometimes think to myself as I go about dealing with issues and problems, *What would Mike recommend?* We miss him every day of our lives and try to keep in mind that he now knows what Jesus has prepared for us and he would not want to come back.

Chapter Twenty

I was reelected to my sixth term as State Senator in November 2002 and, at that time, had served twenty-four years. Pursuant to the rules adopted by the Senate that year, I was named dean of the Senate. The title really didn't mean much other than the honor of the position and being part of the top leadership. One of the best perks of the position was a new office at the front of the hall near the Senate chamber. I had walked the long hall from 1986 when we moved from the old capitol building into the renovated state highway department building across the street, which was later named the Alabama State House.

When we were at the capitol, only a few senators had an office. Most of us had only a desk somewhere in a committee room, but my second term, I became a committee chairman and was given an office on the third floor to share with another senator. The old capitol building was literally about to fall in on us due to lack of maintenance over the years. It had seen over one hundred years of changes in the function of state government and was no longer able to provide the necessary space and convenience required for today's capitol building.

The legislature had operated in the Alabama State House building on Union Street at that time for twenty-three years. It seems like yesterday when we moved into it and all the senators got a private office. It was so much better than before, especially when we had visitors from our districts come to Montgomery to see us. Although the offices were small, they give us a place to talk with people in private.

There have been discussions about building a new state legislative building to meet the needs of expanding government, but I think if that happens, it will probably be several years away. However, someday a governor and legislature will have to face this issue.

Over the years, we learned (as the saying goes) to "make do with what we have." I know most voters don't believe this, but I can assure them that the State of Alabama funds its state agencies less than any other state per capita, and we have the lowest tax burden than any other state.

These days, the word conservative can mean several different things, but I'm talking about taxing, spending, saving, and borrowing money. One of the greatest things we do here in our state is we cannot spend more money than we take in. Our federal government could use our way of funding government.

Bobby speaking in the Senate

My work at Northwest Shoals Community College had been going well for several years. The foundation was successful in raising funds to provide scholarships for students. The community of Northwest Alabama had accepted the college, and much good was being done. Through the leadership of then president of the college, Dr. Larry McCoy, and the help of one of our foundation board members, Perry Bigbee, a new modern gym was constructed. Perry Bigbee and his family founded Bigbee Steel Buildings of Muscle Shoals, and with their help, we were able to build a building worth more than a million dollars for a few hundred thousand dollars. I remember my dear friend and former president of the foundation, Bob Downie, signing the note with me at First Metro Bank. I wondered what would happen should the foundation not be able to repay this loan. Bob Downie passed away in 2006, and the Shoals community suffered a great loss.

I loved my job at the college and all the people I worked with, but after serving in the Senate and carrying out my duties for the college and foundation for all those years, I began to consider retirement. When I turned sixty-five years old, I had been employed at the college for nineteen years. I had finely begun saving money over the last several years. Barbara, and I did the math and decided it may be time for me to take another big step in our lives and leave a job again. So, I retired from Northwest Shoals Community College in 2003, and this time, I believe the decision was a good one. The only thing I truly miss is the people who worked with me.

After our son Mike's death, I began looking into the problem of staph infections. Right away, I learned that there are thousands of cases each year all over the country and many here at home. I began to ask questions about how one would know if they were in a safe environment in the hospitals and medical facilities. I learned that there were no official records or reporting systems in place for these facilities to allow the public to know which have good or bad records with infections. The State of Alabama did not have a law requiring hospitals to keep records and report infections. I also learned there were over twenty-five other states that did have laws regarding this, but they really didn't do anything of substance to help the situation.

After a long battle, I finally passed a bill to change the way this matter is handled in Alabama. My colleagues in the legislature named the law in honor of my son Mike, so the new law is named *"The Mike Denton Infection Reporting Act."*

I worked with the *Alabama Hospital Association* diligently to develop this legislation, which will make a difference in this life-or-death matter. My bargaining tool was that I had lost a son, and about 99,000 others around the country lose loved ones every year. This was an issue that the public could relate to. The federal government should have already passed legislation to require every hospital and medical facility to operate under the same procedures, but I'm sure the Congress would face even more opposition than I have trying to get the state law passed.

Without a law, the hospitals were dealing with public rumors regarding staph infections. When a patient was infected, they would tell everyone what hospital they were in, and the public would seek other places to have treatment. This is not good because a lot of people are convinced that the small local hospitals are the only hospitals that have a problem. That's not true; the big hospitals have many cases also.

If one would just consider how we regulate our other public establishments it becomes easier to understand why we needed a law to deal with infections. Every restaurant, beauty salon, and barbershop have health ratings posted on the wall for public view. This is the law for them, and just about everyone is proud we have that law. The fastest way for one of these places to go out of business is to have a low score reported on the six o'clock news for their customers to see.

The hard-fought process of passing legislation is very frustrating. At times, we feel like it may not be worth the effort because most of the people don't know what is involved, and some of them don't even care. But I have always believed that leaders should try their best to do what they can do for the overall good of the public we serve. Now I'm so happy that Alabama finally has a law that may save lives in the years to come.

Chapter Twenty-one

Barbara's mother developed congestive heart failure, and the doctor said she may not survive the condition for more than a year or two. However, she managed to live with it for more than ten years. Later, Mamaw developed a major blockage of her intestines, and this required a very serious operation. At her age, we were worried about her.

The surgeon removed the affected area and installed a colostomy, and this was a terrible experience for her and the family. After the surgery, her first question to a doctor was, "Is it possible to have this procedure reversed?"

The doctor said it could be after about a year if she did well otherwise, but it would be a very serious operation. She was very self-conscious, as anyone would be, and needed help with it each day. She lived in an apartment in Tuscumbia alone at the time, so one of the daughters, Barbara and Carolyn, or the family angel, Julie, would come to her apartment and help her with the colostomy bag.

As the months went by, she would remind the doctor that she wanted the reversal done as soon as possible. So, in six months she checked into the hospital and had the surgery. It was very hard on her at her age, and she had a few close calls. After she went home, we all kept close watch on her, and one of the girls stayed with her overnight for a few days. We also arranged for her to have an emergency call device she could wear as a necklace, but she never wanted to use it. Later, as she healed well, we got a woman to come and live with her around the clock.

It seems these days we live in now are so different than when my grandparents were old and stayed with members of the family. Now everyone has a job, and there is always a reason we cannot keep our loved ones in our homes anymore. This has created a very large industry in our society called assisted living. If a person does not qualify for Medicaid, he or she cannot be accepted in a nursing home without the extremely high price of private pay.

Alabama has the poorest Medicaid funding program in the nation. Mamaw did not qualify for Medicaid because her social security check of just over $600 a month was too much. So that meant the family was responsible for all her medicine and the medical cost not covered by Medicare, which covers most of the hospital and doctor charges for people over sixty-five. For someone who only receives just over $600 a month to be denied Medicaid is absolutely ridiculous!

We could see Mamaw was not completely happy staying at home with the woman living with her. She needed a better situation than that. We research all the assisted living facilities around the area and found the perfect one for her. Wellington Place, now named (The Pearl) was a new facility and was located within a mile from our home in Muscle Shoals. The people were very nice and cared for her like she was their own mother. The place was very clean, and the food was excellent. Wellington Place offered all kinds of programs for the residents, including exercise, games, live entertainment, and church services. She was happy in her new private room with all her cherished things from home around her.

I loved Mamaw like she was my own mother; after all I had known her much longer than I did my own sweet mother, who gave birth to me and cared for me in ways that I will never know. Barbara's mother was happy at Wellington Place, and we never regretted a penny of the money it cost for her to live there. Barbara and her sister Carolyn shared the cost beyond her little monthly social security check to pay Wellington Place, and we all provided for any other needs she had.

Each week when the Senate was in session and Barbara and I went to Montgomery, Mamaw always worried about our traveling on the highway. I can hear her now saying, "Y'all be careful."

Over the years, she had been like my parents when it came to uttering the words "I love you." She just didn't ever say it; however, she began to change during the last several years and said it often, and we always said it to her. I cannot remember a time after a visit with her or at the end of a telephone conversation that she didn't end the conversation with, "I love you." We all use this affectionate salutation now as we communicate with family members and even others who we feel fondly toward.

The term "I love you" will melt a heart of steel and can change a person's life. It is also very contagious to others. I have used the words in ending a phone conversation with people I like and think the world of, but some of them just can't say, "I love you too." With some, the best you can ever get back from them is, "You too."

When I said that to my brother Buddy he would always say, "OK." Some men may think it's sissy to say such a thing to another man, although they both know that they loved the other.

We all love people without being in love with them. I love my neighbors, but I'm not in love with them. "I love you" are the sweetest three words one can ever say to another person. Of course, we should never go around using the words loosely or flippantly. But I can assure you that using these words to the right people at the right time will help you and them.

When we realized the time had come for Mamaw to take her heavenly flight, we were all in her room as she slowly drifted away in death. I again thought about the angels who were there and could not be seen. It was March 12, 2008, at 6:30 p.m.

The staff at Wellington Place had prepared food and coffee for the family while we waited with her. Barbara, Carolyn, and Julie read several scriptures to her during her last hours and took turns lying beside her on the bed. Mamaw was eighty-six years old and always looked so pretty, with her nails polished and her hair styled nicely. The funeral was beautiful and conducted in a manner she would have wanted.

She was laid to rest at the Tuscumbia Oakwood Cemetery by her husband, Eugene, and next to her beloved grandson Mike.

Again, love lifted us out of the valley of death and sorrow. Through faith, we are assured we shall see our loved ones again someday. That love also allows us to recall the fond memories of them, and through our faith, we realize that, someday, we will take this journey into eternity ourselves. While we are alive here on earth, we have the choice regarding where we will spend eternity.

Chapter Twenty-two

I had begun developing back trouble in the early '80s and tried almost everything to alleviate the pain. For a long time, my best results came through my longtime friend and chiropractor Jerry Plexco. Jerry helped me a lot and kept me going for years until I had my first back surgery in 1981.

Over the ensuing years, I have undergone five back surgeries, a disc fusion surgery in my neck, and surgery for normal-pressure hydrocephalus. NPH is a neurological condition that usually affects people over fifty-five years old. It is an accumulation of cerebrospinal fluid causing the ventricles of the brain to enlarge and stretching the nerve tissue. A quarter million Americans with some of the same symptoms as dementia, Alzheimer's, or Parkinson's may actually have NPH like I did.

This fluid is necessary to cushion the delicate brain and spinal cord from injury. Normally, the bloodstream absorbs most of the fluid produced on a daily basis. Every day our body produces a certain amount; if that amount is excessive, then, over time, the brain will be affected, causing the normal-pressure hydrocephalus.

A surgical procedure has been developed over the years to allow doctors to implant a shunt device between the skull and the skin and then make a small hole in the skull and insert a tube into the brain. The tube coming from the other end of the shunt is directed through the fatty tissue of the body just under the skin and passing down below the abdominal cavity where the excessive fluid will be absorbed.

Barbara stayed with me night and day and helped me through it all. She has always been there for me, in sickness or in health, for better or for worse, for richer or for poorer.

As we grow older and reflect back on our lives, it's exactly as Solomon in the Bible describes the things we have considered to be important—things like making money, popularity, power, and tons of other things. He said, in the end, it's all vanity. Our relationship with God, our fellow man, and our family are the real things we should be concerned about because all the other things will not matter.

Has anyone actually known and talked to a person beyond a grandparent or a great-grandparent in the family tree? I don't believe there are many who have. The cemeteries are packed with graves of great people, but we have never met them. Some may have been famous, and we have read about them and the life they lived. They are quickly forgotten by most people beyond the immediate family members.

We have so many blessings to be thankful for, and it's impossible to know them all, just as we can't remember the times our mother cared for us and protected us from harm as a baby; the long nights she rocked us while we were sick; or the hard, long days our fathers worked to provide for the needs of our family. These things are very important and are the only real things we can appreciate for the rest of our lives.

Chapter
Twenty-three

In 2013 our daughter, Julie, developed a severe headache, and Philip carried her to the hospital. After an MRI of her head, the doctors discovered six large spots in her brain. They were shocked and could not believe what they saw and immediately thought it had to be cancer.

Julie's condition began to worsen by the hour, and no one knew what to do. Several doctors came to her room and expressed regrets but did nothing.

Later, a cardiologist who is a friend of ours saw Phil and me standing in the hallway and asked what we were doing at the hospital. We told him about Julie and that no one was helping her. He went to the nurse's desk to look at her chart and said, "We have to get her out of here fast." He began arranging to fly her to Huntsville Hospital.

The helicopter came, and she was taken to Huntsville—already in an unconscious condition.

Upon arrival, she was put on life support while arrangements were made to do exploratory surgery as soon as possible. The neurosurgeon reviewed her MRI and determined that only one of the spots (whatever they were) could be reached and possibly removed. So he proceeded to do surgery on the side of her head, opening her skull to reach the spot.

Waiting for the doctor to complete the operation, which took a very long time, was terrifying.

When the doctor came out to talk with us, we were in horror wondering what he had found. The doctor said, "I removed the object, and it is not cancer because it is not a tumor; it is a mass of infection that I have never seen in a brain before."

We were somewhat relieved but continued to be very worried about the five remaining spots inside her brain, which were each the size of a grape.

An infectious disease specialist was called in. The specialist started Julie on massive amounts of antibiotics and sent a specimen to Mayo Clinic for evaluation and suggestions as to what could be done.

Mayo Clinic responded quickly with the recommendation of an antibiotic, the same one the doctor at Huntsville was already giving her.

Julie remained on life support for a few days and then began to slowly recover in a very grave condition. The doctors researched and found that only a very few cases of this type of brain infection had ever been discovered. She slowly improved over the next several days and was admitted to the rehab hospital next door. She had a long stay in rehab and had to learn to walk and talk again. Philip stayed by her side for the entire time as she worked hard to get back to normal. The family and friends all prayed, thanking God for helping her through the near-death ordeal.

Later as we thought things were getting better for the family, Julie fell while getting off her riding lawn mower and broke her shoulder. She went through a long period of time recovering from the surgery. And then within a few months, the other shoulder had to be replaced. We felt so sorry for her because she has always been the one who helped other members of our family with problems.

Then within a year it was unbelievable that she violated one of the most important rules for driving that I had given all the children when teaching them to drive. It was "running off the pavement and overreacting." Julie met a truck pulling a wide trailer at the top of a steep hill on the narrow road near their house. The trailer was over the center line and about to hit her car. Julie ran off the pavement to avoid hitting the trailer and over corrected, causing her to wreck, crashing into a rocky embankment beside the road. The impact totaled her car and crushed her left foot and ankle into pieces. She has undergone several related surgeries over the years

My daughter, Julie

My God and I

Chapter Twenty-three

The first week of December 2017, while we were sitting at home talking, Barbara said to me, "Bobby, I have a weird feeling in my chest."

I asked if she had any pain in her neck or arms.

"No," she said. "It's just an aching feeling in the middle of my chest."

I told her we should go to the doctor and get it checked. We had both had a stress test a few months before, and Barbara's test hadn't revealed any problems. However, the doctor had found that I had a condition called A-fib, and I'd been prescribed a blood thinner to take while I waited to have surgery to correct the irregular heartbeat.

The next day, we went to see the cardiologist again. He ran a different test and sent her to Huntsville in an ambulance to have an arteriogram to check for blockages.

After the arteriogram, the doctor came into the room where the children and I were waiting and said to us, "Barbara has a blockage of 90 to 95 percent in all arteries leading to her heart. She also has severe blockage in both carotid arteries in her neck." He said he didn't know how she was living in that condition.

This was terribly shocking news to hear. I was crushed and could not believe it. My dear wife had always taken care of me and the children and had never been sick; this just couldn't be happing. "Oh, God, please help her."

Then I thought that it could work out because we saw people all the time who, after having heart surgery, were walking around in a day or two. *Maybe she will get through this serious problem and be all right*, I told myself. I was very wrong!

When Barbara was going into the operating room, she was smiling and looked so beautiful. We all hugged her and said that we loved her. I said, "Honey, I love you, and I'll see you after a while." She was in surgery for seven hours and came out of the operating room on life support. I was out of my mind and felt helpless. She was placed in the critical ICU unit. That day went by and then the next day and the next while the doctor continued giving us hope.

Barbara stayed on the ventilator while my children and I waited around the clock and prayed hard for God to help her. Julie and Roger went with me time after time to the little chapel while I prayed loudly to God for help. I prayed sitting, kneeling, and lying flat on the floor.

After fifteen days, an assistant of the doctor came to the room near the ICU unit where we were waiting. The young man said, "The doctor said she would not be able to recover and they will be removing the life support."

I thought, *Oh no! Dear God, this cannot be real.*

The young man came back to the room in just a few minutes and said, "She passed away at 8:30 p.m." He didn't say I'm sorry or anything else.

The surgeon who we had seen and talked with several times each day for two weeks never came and said I'm sorry. Nobody said I'm sorry! I had just lost the one who I had loved almost all my life and nobody said I'm sorry! I believe doctors must think that saying they are sorry would be an admission of guilt.

Barbara and I had been married sixty years and exactly one month and still were very much in love.

As I remember all the years we spent together and the good and bad times we went through, I am reminded of the beautiful old gospel song *"My God and I"* written by Austris A. Wiltol in 1932. I recorded it in 1976 in an album of gospel songs used as a fund raiser for the Alabama Music Hall of Fame. The words are so simple and meaningful:

> *My God and I go in the fields together*
> *We walk and talk as good friends should and do;*
> *We clasp our hands, our voices ring with laughter*
> *My God and I walk through the meadow's hue.*
> *This earth will pass and with-it common trifles*
> *But God and I will go unendingly.*

It was December 23, 2017, when the angels came for her. I had always thought I would be the one who would go first. I had everything arranged for her in a file to help her know about our finances and other matters.

Barbara was a good God-loving person, and there is no question regarding where she is now. As I now live alone, I continue to often think she's still here with me. The experience of losing my wife has been the hardest thing to deal with in all my life. Now I can only hope that *My God and I* will continue on with the memories of her until the angels come for me.

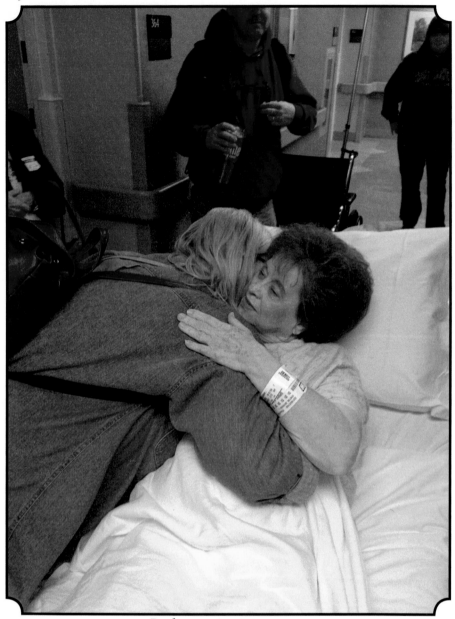

Barbara going into surgery